Walter Monroe

Experimental chemistry for high school students

Walter Monroe

Experimental chemistry for high school students

ISBN/EAN: 9783337156725

Printed in Europe, USA, Canada, Australia, Japan

Cover: Foto ©Paul-Georg Meister /pixelio.de

More available books at **www.hansebooks.com**

EXPERIMENTAL CHEMISTRY

FOR

HIGH SCHOOL STUDENTS

BY

WALTER MONROE,

Instructor in Chemistry in the Monrovia High School

MONROVIA, CALIFORNIA,
1899

PREFACE.

THIS course of experiments has been arranged for students in high schools, and is intended to lead directly to the courses in the State University. Since many of the principles of chemistry are founded upon quantitative relations, a number of such experiments has been introduced; but no exercise has been incorporated into the course that has not been successfully performed. Special care has been taken in clearly describing the experiments, so that pupils may not fail to obtain good results. Considerable attention has also been given by questions and suggestions to cause the student to think carefully over observed phenomena.

The use of symbols has been avoided in the earlier stages of the work, and qualitative analysis has been entirely omitted. Very little of real value can be accomplished in the way of qualitative analysis in so short a time.

A number of the most important elements and their compounds has been considered, and the experiments outlined are only those which may be performed by the student during the year. The course may be modified, whenever desirable, by supplementary directions prepared by the instructor. The writer is of the opinion that a few elements and their most important compounds studied carefully, are of much more value than a great many studied hurriedly.

The exercises are intended to develop in the pupil a

"scientific habit of thought" and lead him to discover for himself by a purely inductive method many of the fundamental principles of the science.

A course of recitations, and an occasional lecture illustrated by experiments should accompany the laboratory work. The note-book should be used in the laboratory only, so that it may always represent the pupil's own thoughts.

Large "folders" with perforated paper that may be removed make the best laboratory note-books. The written sheets may be passed in for examination by the instructor, and afterwards fastened in the folders and kept for future reference.

Very few directions have been given to pupils, for these are best left to the discretion of the teacher.

The writer is indebted to Prof. Rising of the State University for many valuable suggestions. It is likewise a pleasure to acknowledge the assistance received from Mr. Sharwood, formerly of the University, who has so kindly aided in the presentation of the book. Much of the material has been adapted from his course on the "General Laws of Chemical Action."

It was not the intention to have this course put into print until next year; but the demand for the work by a number of instructors has induced the author to have a limited number printed for use this year. Next year the book will appear in better form, and with it a text book which is now in preparation and especially adapted to the course. Further suggestions from the instructors in chemistry at the University, and from teachers who may use the book the coming year will be thankfully received.

WALTER MONROE.

Monrovia, Cal., June 15, 1899.

CONTENTS.

PART I.

THE NON-METALS AND THEIR COMPOUNDS.

EXP. NO.

1	Physical and Chemical Changes.
2	Mechanical Mixture and Chemical Compound.
3–5	Oxygen, Preparation and Properties.
6–9	Hydrogen, Preparation and Properties.
10–13	Water.
14	Estimation of Water in Copper Sulphate.
15	{ Volumetric Measurement of Gases. { Equivalent Weight of Zinc and Magnesium.
16	Nitrogen, Preparation and Properties.
17	Composition of the Atmosphere.
18	Ammonia, Preparation and Properties.
19	Nitrous Oxide, " " "
20	Nitric Oxide, " " "
21	Nitric Acid, " " "
22	Hydrochloric Acid, Preparation and Properties.
23	Chlorine, " " "
24–25	Carbon, " " "
26	Carbon Dioxide, " " "
27	Carbon Monoxide, " " "
28	Flame, Combustion, Heat, Light, etc.
29	Sulphur and Its Properties.
30	Sulphur Dioxide, Preparation and Properties.
31	Hydrogen Sulphide, " " "
32	Sulphuric Acid, " " "
33	Acids, Bases, Salts, etc.
34	Neutralization.

CONTENTS.

PART II.

THE METALS AND THEIR COMPOUNDS.

EXP. NO.

35	Potassium.
36	Potassium Compounds.
37	Sodium.
38	Sodium Compounds.
39	Ammonium Compounds.
40	Calcium Compounds.
41	Zinc.
42	Zinc Compounds.
43–44	Oxidation and Reduction.
45	Iron.
46	Iron Compounds.
47	Copper.
48	Equivalent Weight of Copper.
49	Lead and Its Compounds.
50–51	Silver and Its Compounds.
52	Mercury and Its Compounds.
53	Action of Acids on the Metals.
54	Chlorides.
55	Oxides.
56	Hydroxides.
57	Sulphides.
58	Nitrates.
59	Sulphates.
60	Carbonates.
61	Crystallization.
62	Determination of Atomic Weights.

APPENDIX.

Table of Principal Elements, Atomic Weights and Symbols.
Complete List of Chemicals and Apparatus Required for the Course.
Individual Apparatus.
Preparation of Solutions.
Addresses of Supply Houses.

GENERAL DIRECTIONS.

Students should provide themselves with a towel, some pieces of cloths, and an apron—one with sleeves is the best protection.

Keep your desk in as good order as possible; and before leaving the laboratory, see that your apparatus is clean and the table dry. Never use dirty apparatus. Glass vessels should be cleaned as soon after use as possible, rinsed and left to drain and dry — not wiped unless required for immediate use. No one can do good work in chemistry who neglects these essential points.

Do not put down the stopper when using a re-agent bottle, but hold it between the fingers. Any excess of a re-agent must not be poured back into the re-agent bottle. Always see that your flasks and tubes are dry on the outside before heating, and apply the heat gently at first.

Use great care in handling the strong acids and alkalies. Forceps should be used in handling phosphorus, potassium, and sodium. Do not perform experiments outside of the regular work without permission as serious accidents sometimes occur

Before commencing an experiment, read the directions carefully, and ascertain the object of it. Always ask for information when you are in doubt. The quality of the work done by each student and his ability to draw correct conclusions from observed facts, is of far more value than the bare number of experiments performed.

Watch carefully for changes that may take place, and write in your note-book in the laboratory an account of the experiment as you have performed it, (a sketch of the apparatus will quite often save time in description) and state any conclusions you have been able to draw. Be careful to note everything the experiment shows, and answer all questions fully.

Write the description neatly, accurately, and in good English. Do not use abbreviations for chemicals, but write the name in full. When your instructor performs an experiment, write an account of it just as if you had performed it yourself.

PRELIMINARY WORK.

Make yourself thoroughly familiar with the practical use of the metrical standards, and learn to estimate volumes in cubic centimeters.

Graduate a test tube to measure 5 and 10^{cc} by pouring water from a graduate into the test tube. Mark the level of the water by a small file scratch. For most experiments, not quantitative, the amounts to be taken are merely approximate and may be weighed on paper on a rough balance. Volumes of liquids can be measured in graduated vessels.

Under the direction of your teacher, learn to do the following well:—Bend glass tubing and round the ends, draw out tubing, close the ends of a glass tube, make bulbs, bore corks and fit tubes in them. Always have your apparatus neatly arranged. Ask your teacher to assist you in fitting up apparatus until you become familiar with the work.

PART I.

EXPERIMENTS.

THE NON-METALS AND THEIR COMPOUNDS.

PHYSICAL CHANGE AND CHEMICAL CHANGE.

1. Changes which do not alter the nature or composition of substances are known as physical changes. Ice may change to water and water to steam, but the composition of the substance is unchanged and the changes are physical.

Changes in the nature and composition of substances as well as a change in properties are chemical changes. The burning of wood and the rusting of iron are examples of chemical change.

(a) Dissolve 2 grams of sugar in about 5^{cc} of water. Taste the solution. What change has taken place? Always give reasons for your answers. Add slowly 5^{cc} of concentrated sulphuric acid. Note any change of color, or temperature of the tube. Is there any sugar left? What kind of a change has taken place?

(b) Dissolve a gram of salt in 10^{cc} of water in an evaporating dish. Evaporate to dryness and examine the residue. What is its color and taste? Name the change that took place.

(c) Hold a piece of platinum wire in the flame of your lamp, remove and allow to cool. Repeat with a piece of magnesium ribbon; hold the magnesium with a pair of pincers. What change takes place in each case? Give reasons. Mention other changes similar to these with which you are familiar.

MECHANICAL MIXTURE AND CHEMICAL COMPOUND.

2. (a) Mix intimately about one gram of flowers of sulphur with an equal weight of fine iron filings. Examine the mixture. Can you distinguish the particles of iron and those of sulphur? Examine again with a lens.

(b) Spread some of the mixture on a piece of paper, and pass a magnet over it. What is the effect? The operation may be repeated a number of times if necessary.

(c) Put a small quantity of the mixture in a test tube and cover well with carbon disulphide. (Carbon disulphide is a very volatile liquid and should never be heated.) Shake vigorously several times, and notice whether any change takes place. Filter the substance (ask for directions); catch the filtrate upon a watch glass, and allow it to evaporate. What is left on the filter paper? Allow it to become dry and test with a magnet. What is the color of the substance on the watch glass? What is it? Has the separation of the iron and sulphur been accomplished by physical or chemical processes?

(d) Take all but a small quantity of the mixture and place it in a small ignition tube. Heat strongly for some time and observe closely the changes that take place. After the action is over and the tube is cooled, break it and catch the contents on a piece of paper. Compare the substance with the original mixture. Examine it with the lens, magnet, and carbon disulphide. What kind of a change has taken place?

OXYGEN.

3. (a) Mix intimately, without pulverizing, 25 grams of coarsely powdered potassium chlorate with an equal weight of pure coarsely powdered manganese dioxide. Explosions sometimes occur by using impure manganese dioxide. Test the mixture by heating a little in a test tube. If no violent action takes place, put the mixture in a retort (copper, if obtainable), or a flask, and insert a delivery tube. Heat the retort and fill several receivers (cylinders or wide-mouthed bottles) with the gas by the displacement of water.

(b) Put a lighted splinter into a small receiver; remove it and put it in again while glowing. Does oxygen support combustion? Inhale a little of the gas. What can you say of its odor, taste and appearance?

(c) Put some sulphur into a deflagrating-spoon (a piece of crayon hollowed out and attached to a copper wire will answer) and hold it in one of the receivers. Into another receiver introduce a piece of charcoal; and into a third, a small piece of phosphorus. Let them stand a few minutes, and note any changes that take place.

(d) Repeat with the same elements, but ignite them before introducing into the receivers. How does oxygen act upon substances at ordinary temperatures and at high temperatures?

(e) Fill three test tubes with oxygen and put a piece of dry phosphorus into one, a piece of roll sulphur into another, and a piece of charcoal into the third. Cork the tubes *loosely*, and place them in a beaker of cold water. Heat the water slowly, or pour boiling water slowly into the cold. Observe the changes that take place. Which element has the lowest kindling temperature, and which the highest?

4. It has been found by numerous experiments that whether a substance burns in pure oxygen or in the air, the result is generally the same.

(a) Ask for directions for using the delicate balance, and weigh accurately a porcelain crucible which has been previously heated and allowed to cool, or which has been left in a desiccator for some time. Why? Ask if you do not know.

(b) Take about one-half gram of magnesium ribbon, weigh accurately and place it in the crucible. Place the crucible on a triangle over a flame and heat it until the magnesium is converted into a powder, and then place it in a desiccator and allow it to cool.

(c) Weigh the crucible and contents accurately. How has the magnesium changed in weight? Note any change in appearance, conduct, etc., of the magnesium, and state what the experiment shows.

Lead may be used in this experiment instead of magnesium. Use about a gram; but before weighing, it should be brightened with sandpaper, or have the dark part cut off with a sharp knife. After the lead is melted, it should be stirred continually with a stout iron wire until it ceases to be in a liquid form.

5. (a) Put about one gram of mercuric oxide in a hard glass tube, and insert a delivery tube. Heat the tube to redness if necessary and collect the gas in a test tube or a wide-mouthed bottle over water. Test the gas collected. How do you know what it is? Note any change that has taken place in the mercuric oxide.

(b) Repeat (a) using about four grams of manganese dioxide instead of the mercuric oxide.

HYDROGEN.

6. (a) Place 15 to 20 grams of granulated zinc in a flask or Wolff's bottle; attach a delivery tube, and through a second opening insert a thistle or funnel tube. Add about 100^{cc} of dilute hydrochloric acid or sulphuric acid. What is the effect? Allow time for the air to be expelled from the generator and tube, and then fill several cylinders or bottles with gas by the displacement of water. Fill a test tube with the gas, invert it and bring a lighted match to its mouth. What happens? Light a candle or splinter and introduce it into one of the vessels of gas, having the mouth of the receiver downward. Does hydrogen behave like oxygen?

(b) Take two vessels containing the gas; place one with its mouth upward, the other with its mouth downward. Uncover both vessels and after a few moments introduce a lighted taper into each. Explain the difference.

(c) Take a cylinder or bottle containing air and pour the gas from one of the receivers into it. How must the vessels be held? How can you tell that the gas has been poured from one vessel to the other? What does the experiment show?

(d) Collect some of the gas from the generator after passing it through a bottle containing a solution of potasaium permanganate. Has hydrogen any odor, taste or color? What is the use of the potassium permanganate?

7. (a) Arrange an apparatus as in the previous experiment, but instead of the delivery tube, attach a U-shaped tube filled with calcium chloride. Roll up a piece of platinum foil so as to make a small tube and seal it to one end of a glass tube about 15^{cm} long. Connect the other end of the glass tube to the calcium chloride tube so that the platinum point will be almost in a vertical position.

(b) Add dilute hydrochloric acid and after action has been going on long enough to expel all air, light the hydrogen escaping from the jet. (It is well to test the gas before lighting. How? Ask if you do not know. Wrap a towel around the flask to prevent any serious accident in case of an explosion.) Place a bell-jar or other wide-mouthed vessel over the flame at an angle, and examine after a few minutes. Explain the chemical change that takes place when hydrogen burns in air. What is the use of the calcium chloride tube? Why is the platinum tube used in the end of the glass tube? What is the appearance of the hydrogen flame?

8. (a) Take an iron gas or water pipe about 50^{cm} long and 20^{mm} internal diameter, and fill the middle portion with iron turnings. Fasten the pipe in a horizontal position by means of a clamp attached near one end. Partly fill a flask with water, place it on a ring stand, and connect with one end of the iron pipe. Insert a delivery tube in the other end of the pipe and arrange to collect gas over water. Heat the iron pipe to redness in the center, and boil the water in the flask.

(b) Collect several samples of the gas and test them. What is the gas? Give reasons. After the tube has cooled, examine the iron turnings. Explain the changes that have taken place during the experiment.

9. (a) Fit a porous earthen cup to a glass tube about 25 or 30^{cm} long, having a small internal diameter. (Instead of the porous cup, a plaster of Paris plug may be inserted in the end of the glass tube which may, in this case, be shorter and about 2^{cm} in internal diameter.)

Put the other end of the tube through a cork in one neck of a Wolff's bottle containing some water colored with litmus, or any other coloring matter. Do not pass the tube below the surface of the water. Through the other neck of the bottle pass a small glass tube below the surface of the water. The upper end of this tube should extend above the bottle about 10^{cm}, be bent outward slightly, and drawn out at the end to a small opening.

(b) Fill a bell-jar with dry hydrogen by the displacement of air, and bring it over the porous cup. Note what happens and explain all that you have seen. Does the bell-jar filled with air produce the same effect?

WATER.

10. Procure the apparatus for the electrolysis of water, and pour water into the glass vessel until the platinum electrodes are below the surface. Take two large test tubes of the same size, and fill them with water containing a small amount of sulphuric acid. Invert the test tubes and place them over the platinum electrodes; then pour into the glass vessel about one-twelfth as much strong sulphuric acid as it contains water. Water alone will not conduct a current, but when sulphuric acid is added it acquires the power to convey the current. Connect a battery of two or three cells in series to the copper wires in connection with the platinum electrodes. Notice the electrodes. When the water has been completely forced out of one tube, how full is the other? Test the gas thus collected. How do you know what the gasses are? Which gas collects the faster? In what proportion do the two gasses unite to form water?

11. From the knowledge you already have of the behavior of water, state its boiling and freezing points. At what temperature does it weigh most? What is the weight of one cubic centimeter at that temperature? Is the temperature at which water boils affected by the pressure under which it boils?

(a) Fill a flask of about one liter capacity one-third full of water from the hydrant and connect it with a condenser. Distil about 50 to 100^{cc} of the water and compare it with the hydrant water as to taste, odor and color.

(b) Evaporate to dryness—in a watch glass set over a beaker of water, or in an evaporating dish—about 5^{cc} of the distilled water.

(c) Treat in a similar manner an equal amount of water from the hydrant. Compare results. Could sea water be made fit to drink by distillation?

12. (a) Heat about one gram of copper sulphate crystals in a small test tube. Observe what takes place.

(b) Repeat (a) using one gram of alum.

(c) Treat in a similar manner potassium bichromate crystals and compare with (a) and (b).

(d) Place a few crystals of clear sodium sulphate (Glauber's salt) on a watch glass and leave exposed to the air until the next day.

(e) Treat similarly a few pieces of calcium chloride. Compare with (d).

13. Nearly all substances dissolve more or less in water. Platinum, however, is insoluble. Some liquids are soluble in water in all proportions, some are only partially soluble, while liquids like oils are very slightly soluble. The solubility of a substance depends upon the temperature, but it is always definite for a given temperature. The solubility of solids generally increases with the temperature; but the solubility of gases decreases with an increase of temperature.

(a) Put one gram of powdered potassium chlorate

(weighed on a balance) in a test tube, add three or four cubic centimeters of water and heat to boiling. Examine the solution; allow it to cool and examine again.

(b) Add about 15^{cc} of water and heat till completely clear; cool and compare with (a).

(c) Put 5^{cc} of cold water in a test tube and add a few drops of carbon bisulphide. Shake well and let it stand a few minutes. Examine.

(d) Pour 5^{cc} of water in a test tube and add a few drops of ether. Shake, let stand and examine; add a little more ether, and again examine; finally add 4 or 5^{cc} more and examine again.

(e) Repeat (d) using alcohol instead of ether.

ESTIMATION OF WATER IN COPPER SULPHATE.

14. Dry and weigh a small porcelain crucible. (See directions, Exp. 4.) Introduce into it about a gram of bright crystals of pure copper sulphate, slightly powdered and accurately weighed. Heat in an oven (or on asbestos cloth) for at least an hour at a temperature between 100° and 110° C. Cool in a desiccator and weigh. Heat the crucible and contents again under similar conditions for about half an hour, cool and weigh as before. Continue the heating until you find the weight constant. Now heat over a flame almost to a low red heat for about fifteen minutes; cool in a desiccator and weigh. Calculate the amount of water expelled below 110° C.; also the amount expelled between 110° and low red heat. What fraction is this last quantity of the whole amount of water expelled? Calculate the percentage of water in the blue crystals taken.

(b) Put the dry copper sulphate in a test tube and add a few drops of water. Note any change in appearance and temperature.

VOLUMETRIC MEASUREMENT OF GASES.

It has been found by experiment that the volume of a gas varies with the temperature and pressure as follows:

(a) The volume of a given quantity of dry gas increases $\frac{1}{273}$ part of its volume at zero Centigrade for each rise in temperature of one degree Centigrade. (Law of Charles, also law of Gay-Lussac.) Taking —273 as absolute zero and 273 plus the temperature Centigrade the absolute temperature, the volume varies as the absolute temperature divided by the pressure.

(b) The volume of a confined mass of gas is inversely proportional to the pressure to which it is exposed. The volume times the pressure is equal to a constant (Law of Boyle, also Marriotte's Law). The atmospheric pressure varies with the height above sea-level, but it approximates to that of a column of mercury 760^{mm} high which is taken as the standard.

From the above laws we get the following formula which may be used to determine what volume a gas, measured at one temperature and pressure, would occupy at another:

Let V represent the volume of a given mass of gas at 0° C. and 760^{mm} pressure.

Its volume at 1° C. and 760^{mm} pressure $= V + \frac{1}{273}V$.

Its volume at 2° C. and 760^{mm} pressure $= V + \frac{2}{273}V$.

Its volume at t° C. and 760^{mm} pressure $= V + \frac{t}{273}V = V\left(\frac{273+t}{273}\right)$.

Its volume at t° C. and p^{mm} pressure $= V\left(\frac{273+t}{273}\right)\frac{760}{P}$.

The volume of a gas in contact with water is increased owing to pressure of water vapor. Correction may be made by subtracting from the given barometric pressure the tension of aqueous vapor at the given temperature;

that is, substitute for p. in the formula the observed barometric reading minus the tension of water vapor at the temperature t centigrade.

TENSION OF WATER VAPOR FOR DIFFERENT TEMPERATURES.

Temp. C.	Tension of vapor	Temp. C.	Tension of vapor
0°	4.6 mm	21°	18.49 mm
4°	6.0 "	22°	19.69 "
8°	8.0 "	23°	20.88 "
10°	9.16 "	24°	22.18 "
11°	9.8 "	25°	23.55 "
12°	10.5 "	26°	24.98 "
13°	11.6 "	27°	26.5 "
14°	12.0 "	28°	28.1 "
15°	12.7 "	29°	29.78 "
16°	13.5 "	30°	31.54 "
17°	14.4 "	31°	33.4 "
18°	15.35 "	32°	35.35 "
19°	16.3 "	33°	37.4 "
20°	17.3 "		

PROBLEMS.

(1) 18.2 liters of gas are measured at 0° C. and 760 mm pressure; what would be the volume if measured at 17° C. and 950 mm pressure?

(2) A quantity of oxygen occupies a volume of 1216 cc at 15° C. and 750 mm pressure; what is its volume under standard conditions?

(3) 100 cubic centimeters of hydrogen are measured off at 27° C. and 950 mm pressure; what volume would it occupy at 17° C. and 750 mm pressure?

(4) 200 cc of a gas are measured over water at 20° C.

and 760^{mm} pressure; what volume would the gas occupy measured dry at 0° C. and 760^{mm} pressure?

---

15. (a) Clean a small piece of zinc, approximately .05 grams, and weigh accurately. Place it in a beaker on a ring stand, and introduce a funnel with the mouth covering the zinc—stem upward, but not long enough to reach the mouth of the beaker. Add water until the funnel is completely covered, and insert a test tube, filled with water, over the stem; fasten securely with a wire holder or with a clamp. Then with a pipette or a funnel pour 10^{cc} of concentrated sulphuric acid to the bottom of the beaker, and add a few drops of copper sulphate solution. If the action is very slow, warm slightly. When the zinc has all been dissolved remove the clamp, lower the tube into the beaker, and set the beaker into a basin of cold water and leave until cold. Raise or lower the tube till the level of the liquid is the same inside of the tube as outside. Why? Cover with the thumb while so adjusted, remove and invert. Let the gas escape, and measure the volume of the gas. It is equal to the volume of liquid now required to fill the tube. Fill a Burette with water; take the reading, and then run water from it into the test tube until it is exactly as full as in the beginning when inverted over the funnel. The difference in reading gives the volume of gas. (The Burette is read by noting the level of the lower meniscus of surface.) Read the thermometer and the barometer to get the temperature and pressure, and also find the water vapor tension at this temperature. From these data calculate the volume dry at 0° C. and 760^{mm} pressure. Hence calculate the volume of gas liberated by one gram of zinc. One liter (1000^{cc}) of dry hydrogen under standard conditions has been found by careful experiment to weigh 0.0896 grams nearly. Therefore, calculate the equivalent of zinc; that is, the number of grams of zinc required to yield one gram of hydrogen from sulphuric acid. Compare your results with those of other students.

(b) Repeat the above experiment using hydrochloric acid and a different weight of zinc. Is the final result the same?

(c) Repeat the experiment using .02 grams of magnesium, and sulphuric acid. What is the equivalent weight of magnesium?

NITROGEN.

16. Hollow out one end of a piece of crayon about three ^{cm} long and attach it to a piece of wire. Fasten the wire to the shelf of a pneumatic trough, having water 3 or 4^{cm} above the trough. Have the crayon in an upright position and of such a height that it will reach about half way to the bottom of a large wide-mouthed bottle when the bottle is inverted over it. With a pair of forceps, put a piece of phoshorus, the size of a pea, into the crayon cup. Ignite the phosphorus, and quickly invert the wide-mouthed bottle over it. Allow it to stand until the white fumes disappear. What are these fumes and what becomes of them? Cover the mouth of the bottle with a glass plate, and turn it mouth upward. Note the odor and color of the gas. Test the effect of the gas on a burning splinter, phosphorus, and sulphur, introduced one after the other. Does nitrogen support combustion? Where did it come from?

THE ATMOSPHERE.

The air is a mechanical mixture, of which over

ninety-nine per cent. is oxygen and nitrogen.* Water vapor and carbon dioxide are always found present in varying proportions. Besides these, ammonia and some other gases are usually found in small quantities.

17. (a) Take a piece of glass tubing about 20^{cm} long, closed at one end, and from 10 to 15^{mm} in diameter. Bend the closed end to a right angle making the bend about 5^{cm} long. Slip two small rubber rings over the open end, and drop a piece of phosphorus the size of a pea into the bent portion. Dip the open end into a beaker of water, and suck air out with a rubber tube until the water rises about 3^{cm} in the tube. Adjust the tube until the water is at the same level inside and outside. Why? Mark the mean level by the lower rubber ring, and fasten the tube securely with a clamp. Warm the closed end containing the phosphorus, but not enough to drive the expanded air out of the tube. Let the tube cool after the phosphorus has entirely ceased to act. Pour water over the tube; and after the white fumes have disappeared, adjust the upper rubber ring to indicate the volume of the gas left. Is the volume of the gas greater or less than that of the original air? Why?

(b) Fill the tube, first to one rubber ring and then to the other, with water from a Burette, and note the volume in each case. Calculate the percentage composition of air by volume, assuming it to be composed entirely of oxygen and nitrogen. What previous experiment showed the presence of moisture in the atmosphere?

AMMONIA.

18. (a) Add a few drops of caustic soda solution

---

* In the year 1894, Raleigh and Ramsay discovered that about 1 per cent. of what was supposed to be nitrogen was really a new element which they called Argon, meaning inert substance. Since then other elements have been found in very small quantities.

to a little ammonium chloride in a test tube, warm and notice the odor of the gas given off. Repeat the operation using caustic potash instead of caustic soda.

(b) Mix in a mortar about a gram of quicklime and a gram of ammonium chloride, and note the odor as before. What kind of an odor has ammonia? By what other name is it commonly known? Write equations representing the reactions that took place in each case. (The student is supposed to have had, by this time, some practice in writing equations.)

(c) Mix thoroughly about 25 grams of slaked lime with an equal weight of ammonium chloride. Place the mixture in a flask and attach a delivery tube. Heat the flask gently in a sand bath or over asbestos, and collect three cylinders of the gas by the displacement of air; cover securely with glass plates. The mouths of the receivers should be kept downward throughout the experiment unless otherwise directed, as the gas is very much lighter than air. Try to light the gas as it escapes from the generator. Will ammonia burn? Allow the current of gas from the generator to pass into a beaker of water while the cylinders of gas are being examined.

(d) Note the odor and color of the gas. Into one of the receivers put a piece each of wet blue, and red litmus paper. What change takes place? Introduce a burning candle or splinter into the same receiver. Does the gas support combustion? Invert one of the cylinders with its mouth upward, remove the glass cover, and quickly apply a lighted match. Does the ammonia burn?

(e) Moisten the sides of a dry cylinder with concentrated hydrochloric acid, and place it over the third cylinder of the gas collected, so that the mouths of the two vessels are separated only by the glass cover over the receiver of gas. Remove the glass plate, and observe carefully what takes place. What is formed?

(f) Examine the water into which the gas has been passing. How does it affect litmus paper? Boil some of the solution in a test tube. What gas is given off? How does the solution compare with the laboratory reagent? The ammonia gas should be passed through a cylinder of quicklime or caustic soda to obtain it perfectly dry. Why could not calcium chloride be used?

NITROUS OXIDE.

19. (a) Place 15 to 20 grams of ammonium nitrate in a retort or generating flask, and arrange the apparatus as in the preparation of oxygen. Heat *gently*; and after the air has been expelled, collect three receivers of the gas over warm water. Nitrous oxide is somewhat soluble in cold water. If the flask is heated too fast, some nitric oxide will be formed which takes oxygen from the air to form nitrogen peroxide, No_2. Nitrous oxide may contain some chlorine also. In order to obtain the gas pure, it is usually passed through two Wolff's bottles,—the first containing a warm solution of ferrous sulphate which removes the nitric oxide; the other, containing a warm solution of caustic potash to remove the chlorine.

(b) Note the odor, color, and taste of the gas. Introduce a lighted splinter into one of the receivers. Does the gas support combustion? Put a small piece of phosphorus in a deflagrating spoon, ignite, and introduce into a second receiver of the gas. Introduce burning sulphur into the third receiver. What gas does nitrogen monoxide resemble?

NITRIC OXIDE.

20. (a) Arrange a generating flask, and place in it a quantity of metallic copper. Just cover the copper with water, and then slowly pour concentrated nitric acid through the funnel tube until action begins. What is the color of the gas in the flask at first? What is the color after action has continued for a short time? Collect four cylinders of the gas over water, and observe the color. Allow the nitric oxide from the delivery tube to escape into the air and notice the change. The gas unites with the oxygen of the air to form nitrogen peroxide. Explain the appearance of the colored gas in the flask at the beginning of the experiment.

(b) Introduce a lighted splinter into one of the cylinders of gas. Does the gas support combustion? Does it burn?

(c) Put a small piece of phosphorus into a deflagrating spoon, ignite, and lower into a cylinder of gas. What is the effect?

(d) Repeat (c) using sulphur instead of phosphorus.

NITRIC ACID.

21. Place in a retort 30 grams of sodium nitrate or potassium nitrate, and about 20^{cc} concentrated sulphuric acid. Pass the end of the retort into the neck of a flask, and arrange so that the flask may be surrounded with ice, or so that a stream of water may continually flow over it, (a large test tube may be used instead of the flask. It can be kept cool by immersing in cold water.) Heat the retort gently until the operation is finished. In what form is the nitric acid? What is its odor and color? When pure it is colorless, but it usually contains some of the oxides of nitrogen which give it a yellowish color.

(b) Add a small amount of nitric acid to 4 or 5^{cc} of indigo solution in a test tube, and warm.

(c) Put about 20^{cc} of dilute nitric acid in an evaporating dish, and drop into it some quill clippings or small pieces of silk. Evaporate. What color is imparted to animal substances?

(d) Test the action of nitric acid, both the concentrated and the dilute, (one volume of concentrated acid to three of water) upon the following substances: copper, zinc, tin, lead, iron and magnesium. Put about 5^{cc} of acid into a test tube and then drop in a small piece of the metal to be tested. It is well to arrange as many test tubes as there are metals, and test all at the same time. Do all the metals dissolve? Which one seems to dissolve most readily? In which acid, concentrated or dilute, is action most violent?

(e) Put 2^{cc} of concentrated nitric acid into a test tube and drop into it a small piece of platinum. Warm in a flame, and notice carefully for any change.

(f) Repeat (e) using 3^{cc} of concentrated hydrochloric acid instead of the nitric.

(g) Unite the two acids used in (e) and (f). What is the effect? A combination of the two acids form Aqua Regia. The odor produced is that of chlorine. The nascent chlorine unites with the platinum and platinum chloride is produced. If gold is used, auric chloride is formed.

HYDROCHLORIC ACID.

22 (a) Put 50 grams of common salt in a flask and attach a delivery tube. Insert a thistle, or funnel tube, and add about 75^{cc} of dilute sulphuric acid. Connect the delivery tube to a series of two or three Wolff's bottles about half full of water. Heat the flask gently over asbestos or in a sand bath. When the air has been displaced, the gas will be absorbed as soon as it comes in contact with the water. Write the equation which shows the reaction that takes place. After the gas has passed for fifteen to twenty minutes, disconnect the flask from the Wolff's bottles. What do you notice? Blow your breath on the escaping gas. What effect has this? Why? Try to light the gas at the end of the tube. Will it burn?

(b) Fill two wide-mouthed bottles with hydrochloric acid gas by extending the delivery tube to the bottom of the bottle which should be loosely covered with a glass plate or a piece of cardboard. Note the color of the gas. Is it transparent? Drop a moist piece of blue litmus paper into one of the bottles. What is the nature of the gas? Insert a burning splinter or a candle into the bottle. Does the gas support combustion?

(c) Take the second bottle of gas, hold the glass cover securely, and invert the bottle bringing the mouth under water in a beaker or evaporating dish. Remove the glass plate. What happens? Explain. Test the water with blue litmus. Taste the water. Why cannot this gas be collected over water like hydrogen and oxygen? Why was it not necessary to invert the bottles when collecting the gas?

(d) Examine the liquid in the first Wolff's bottle. How does it affect litmus paper? Put about a gram of granulated zinc into a test tube and add about 10^{cc} of the liquid. What is the effect? What gas is given off? Compare the liquid with the laboratory hydrochloric acid. Are they the same?

Hydrobromic acid and hydriodic acid are very much like hydrochloric acid, and are made in the same way. Give the equations representing their preparation.

CHLORINE.

23. This experiment should be performed in the hood or out of doors. Be careful not to inhale the gas given off.

(a) Arrange a flask like the one used in the last experiment, and put in it about 30 grams of manganese dioxide. Pour through the funnel tube about 50^{cc} of hydrochloric acid—enough to cover the manganese dioxide completely. Heat the flask gently as in the last experiment, and fill six cylinders or wide-mouthed bottles with the gas by downward displacement of the air. As the chlorine gas collects, the quantity can be noted by means of the color. What is the color? Write the equation representing the action. (Sulphuric acid could be used instead of hydrochloric acid if an equal weight of common salt be added to the manganese dioxide. Write the equation). After the bottles are full, try to light the gas escaping from the generator. Will it burn? Allow the escaping gas to run into a receiver of water while you are testing the gas collected in the wide-wouthed bottles. Is the gas soluble in water? What is the color of chlorine water? Save the solution. Pour it into a bottle, cork, and set in a place protected from bright light.

(b) 1. Into one of the vessels containing chlorine put some pieces of red and blue litmus paper; a red rose; a green leaf; a piece of cotton print; a piece of newspaper; and a piece of paper with some writing on it. The substances used must be moist. Use two vessels of chlorine if necessary.

2. Put some of the dry articles into another receiver of chlorine. In a short time examine the substances in the receivers, and observe the effect upon each.

3. Lower a lighted candle or taper into a receiver of chlorine. Does the gas support combustion?

4. Warm a little oil of turpentine in an evaporating dish, moisten a piece of filter paper or blotting paper with it, and quickly introduce into a receiver of chlorine. Observe what happens.

5. Sprinkle into another receiver of chlorine a little finely powdered copper, antimony, or arsenic; and observe the effect.

6. Arrange a hydrogen generator as in experiment 7. (Observe the caution). When the air has all been expelled, light the hydrogen and bring the burning jet into the remaining receiver of chlorine. Does it continue to burn? What is formed?

(c) Put about 5^{cc} of indigo solution into a test tube and add 5^{cc} of chlorine water. Do you notice any change? Treat in the same way 5^{cc} of potassium bichromate solution. Note—Teachers should explain, as far as possible, the changes which take place in this experiment.

The preparation of bromine and iodine is similar to the preparation of chlorine. The apparatus used is the same as that used in the preparation of nitric acid. The bromine condenses in the receiver, and forms a reddish liquid. Iodine forms a sublimate of a violet color. Write equations illustrating the reactions that take place when bromine and iodine are made.

CARBON.

24. (a) Hold a plate or piece of porcelain in the flame of a candle, or of a Bunsen burner with the air supply shut off. Observe the color of the deposit. This is an impure form of carbon. What name is given to this particular form of the element? Hold the deposit in the flame of an alcohol lamp, or in a Bunsen flame with the valve at the base of the burner open. Does the deposit disappear? Is carbon a combustible element?

(b) Put some pieces of wood into a small Hessian crucible and cover them with sand. Heat the crucible strongly, and when smoking stops, cool, remove the contents, and examine. This is impure carbon also. What name is given to it? What became of the other products of the wood? Name other forms of the element carbon.

(c) Put about 2 grams of sugar into a porcelain evaporating dish and heat till the sugar is black. Sugar is composed of the elements carbon, hydrogen, and oxygen; when the sugar is heated, water passes off and the carbon is left. The carbon can be removed from the evaporating dish with a strong solution of sodium hydrate.

(d) Place a few grains of sugar into an evaporating dish, and add a few drops of concentrated sulphuric acid. What results? Try starch in the same way.

(e) Test the solubility of carbon (use charcoal) in water, acids, alkalies and alcohol.

(f) Heat some powdered charcoal on a piece of platinum foil. What occurs?

25. (a) Arrange a bone-black filter by placing a paper filter into a funnel and adding bone-black. Filter a dilute solution of indigo and examine the filtrate. Is there any change in the appearance of the solution? Filter in the same way a dilute solution of litmus.

(b) The same effect may be produced by putting bone-black into the solution, boiling for a short time, and then filtering through a paper filter. Try this with any solution colored with animal or vegetable coloring matter; as cochineal, indigo, litmus, iodine. Take about 50^{cc} in a beaker and place in it about one or two grams of bone-black; heat for a short time, shake well and filter.

(c) Pour 10 or 15^{cc} of hydrogen sulphide solution

into a beaker, and note the odor. Add about a gram of bone-black; warm the solution a few moments, shake well and filter. Note the odor again.

(d) Collect over mercury in a test tube some ammonia gas, made by heating a strong solution of ammonia and passing it over quick-lime to dry it. Heat a piece of charcoal; and, without removing the inverted receiver of gas, press it through the mercury into the mouth of the receiver. What is the result? Why was the charcoal heated before introducing it into the test tube?

(e) Mix together 3 or 4 grams of powdered copper oxide, CuO, and about one gram of powdered charcoal; heat strongly for some time in an ignition tube. What remains in the tube? What gas is given off? Write the equation which shows the reaction that takes place. Is carbon an oxidizing or a reducing agent? (The gas given off may be collected by attaching a delivery tube before heating the mixture.) After the tube has become cool, pour in a little strong nitric acid. What takes place? State some of the uses of carbon which have been illustrated by the experiments you have performed.

CARBON DIOXIDE.

26. (a) Put some small pieces of marble (calcium carbonate), 15 or 20 grams, into a generating flask, and pour dilute hydrochloric acid on them through the funnel tube. After action has continued for a time, pass the gas into a test tube of lime-water. Is there any change in appearance? Note the odor and color of the gas. Try to ignite it as it escapes from the delivery tube. Will carbon dioxide burn?

(b) Collect two or three cylinders (or bottles) full of the gas by downward displacement. Into one of the cylinders of gas introduce successively a lighted candle or burning taper, and a small piece of phosphorus in a deflagrating spoon. Pour a cylinder of the gas, as you would water, over a burning splinter. Does the gas support combustion? Is it heavier than air?

(c) Pass the gas from the generator into a test tube containing distilled water; after a short time, taste the water. Test it with litmus paper.

(d) Pass the gas for about ten minutes into a test tube containing a solution of caustic potash; then add hydrochloric acid to the solution. What gas is given off? Write equations representing what has taken place.

(e) Pass the gas into clear lime-water as in the beginning of the experiment, but allow the action to continue for a much longer period. Remove the delivery tube and heat the solution. State the changes that you have observed; and if you do not understand all of them, ask for an explanation.

(f) Blow your breath through a clear solution of lime-water by means of a piece of glass tubing. What is formed?

CARBON MONOXIDE.

27. (a) Put about ten grams of oxalic acid crystals, $H_2C_2O_4$, into a flask; add about 50^{cc} of concentrated sulphuric acid, and connect the flask with a Wolff's bottle containing a solution of caustic soda. Attach a delivery tube to the other neck of the bottle.

(b) Heat the flask gently and collect some of the gas in a test tube over water. Avoid inhaling the gas as it is poisonous. Observe its color. Try to set fire to the gas. Will it burn, or is it a supporter of combustion? Sulphuric acid has great affinity for water, and so it withdraws hydrogen and oxygen from the oxalic acid in the right proportion to form water. The carbon and oxygen combine to form carbon dioxide and carbon monoxide. What becomes of the carbon dioxide?

(c) Repeat (c) in Experiment 26, using carbon monoxide instead of carbon dioxide.

(d) Put some copper oxide into a small hard glass tube open at both ends. Support the tube in a horizontal position and connect one end with the delivery tube from the caustic soda solution. Heat the copper oxide and pass the carbon monoxide over it for a short time. Explain the changes that take place. Is carbon monoxide an oxidizing or a reducing agent?

Problem:—How much carbon monoxide is given off by the decomposition of 10 grams of oxalic acid crystals?

FLAME.

28. (a) Place a lighted candle in front of some dark object and examine the flame closely. Notice its shape, and see how many parts you can distinguish. Make drawings.

(b) Hold a plain white card, or piece of smooth white pine, horizontally in the flame of a candle so that it nearly touches the wick. Remove it before it becomes ignited and hold the other side in a vertical position against the wick. Repeat the experiment until you obtain a vertical section and a transverse section well outlined on the card. Make drawings of each section. Does combustion take place in all parts of the flame?

*(c) Light the gas of a Bunsen burner and examine the flame as you did the candle flame under (a). Has the flame the same number of parts? Obtain several small pieces of soft pine, and hold them successively in a

---
* Omit sections (c), (d) and (e) if Bunsen burners are not used in the laboratory.

horizontal position in the flame and try to determine in what part the combustion is most complete.

(d) Insert a glass tube into the inner cone of the Bunsen flame; slant the tube upward, and apply a lighted match to the upper end. Is a flame produced? What is the effect of placing the glass tube in other parts of the flame?

(e) Bring a piece of wire gauze down upon the flame of a Bunsen burner. What is the effect? Is there any change produced after holding the gauze in the same position for some time? Turn off the gas, then turn it on again without lighting; hold the gauze about 5^{cm} above the burner and see if you can light the gas above it. Explain all the phenomena observed. This experiment represents the principle upon which the miner's safety lamp (called the Davy safety lamp) is constructed.

(f) Notice which portion of the Bunsen (or alcohol) flame is the most luminous. Sprinkle some dry sawdust or powdered charcoal in the flame. Is the illuminating power of the flame greater or less than before? Does it appear to remain constant? Close the openings at the base of the Bunsen burner. How does it change the light of the flame? What are the openings for? What seems to be the cause of light in the flame? State any additional points you can in regard to the combustion, kindling point, heat, and light of flame.

SULPHUR.

29. (a) What is the color, taste and odor of sulphur? Test the solubility of the element in water, alkalies, acids, alcohol and carbon bisulphide.

(b) Put a few grams of sulphur in a Hessian or porcelain crucible; heat until the sulphur is melted, and then allow it to cool slowly. As soon as a crust forms on the surface of the sulphur, make a hole through it and pour out the liquid. Examine carefully the crystals attached to the crust and to the inside of the crucible. What is the shape of the crystals?

(c) Dissolve one or two grams of powdered roll sulphur in a little carbon bisulphide. Put the solution in an evaporating dish or beaker, and allow it to evaporate in the atmosphere. Examine the sulphur crystals. Have they the same shape as those formed in (b)?

(d) Put in a retort a small amount of sulphur, and pass the end of the retort into the neck of a flask. Heat the sulphur to boiling, and after a time examine the sulphur that has collected in the flask. It is called flowers of sulphur.

(e) Put some sulphur into a test tube and heat slowly till it melts. Observe the color of the liquid. Continue the heating and notice carefully any changes that take place. When it becomes a thin liquid, pour a little into an evaporating dish containing water. Allow the heating to go on until the liquid begins to boil, and then pour some more into cold water.

Sulphur boils at about 450° and just above this point it takes fire. Take the two deposits out of the water and examine them; replace them in the water and after they have remained for some time, examine again. Do you notice any change?

What is formed when sulphur burns in oxygen?

SULPHUR DIOXIDE.

30. (a) Note the color and odor of the substance formed when sulphur burns in air.

Put some pieces of sheet copper or copper filings into

a generating flask, and add enough concentrated sulphuric acid to cover them. Heat the flask gently and collect two cylinders of the gas by downward displacement of the air. What is the color of the gas? Has it an odor? Avoid inhaling much of the gas.

(b) Introduce a lighted splinter into the mouth of one of the receivers. Does sulphur dioxide support combustion? Put some moist pieces of litmus paper in a receiver of the gas. What is the effect?

(c) Pass some of the gas into a beaker containing water. Is the gas soluble in water? Examine the water and test it with litmus. What are its properties?

(d) Put a gram or two of sulphur in a porcelain crucible and place it under a tripod or other support upon which are placed as many of the following things as may be had: moist flowers, green leaves, a piece of white woolen yarn, a ripe apricot (or peach) cut in halves, a piece of moistened unbleached silk. Ignite the sulphur and place a large bell-jar over it so as to enclose the articles on the tripod. Leave undisturbed until the fumes settle and then examine. What change takes place in the substances?

(e) A solution of sulphur dioxide in water forms sulphurous acid, H_2SO_3. If left in contact with the air, it combines with oxygen and is converted into sulphuric acid, H_2SO_4. It has the power of taking oxygen from other substances also. Is it an oxidizing or a reducing agent? Add a little of the sulphurous acid obtained in (c) to a solution of potassium permanganate or potassium bichromate containing a little sulphuric acid. What change is noticeable?

HYDROGEN SULPHIDE.

31. (a) Put a few pieces of iron sulphide, FeS, in a generating flask, and pour enough dilute sulphuric acid through the funnel tube to cover them. Write the equation representing the reaction.

(b) Collect some of the hydrogen sulphide by the displacement of air. Make the necessary tests to enable you to answer the following questions: 1. What is its odor and color? 2. Will it burn? 3. Will it support combustion? 4. Is it soluble in water? 5. Is it acid or alkaline?

(c) Place in different test tubes 5^{cc} of each of the following solutions: Copper sulphate, $CuSO_4$; lead nitrate, $Pb(NO_3)_2$; mercuric chloride, $HgCl_2$; arsenic chloride, $AsCl_3$; antimony chloride, $SbCl_3$; stannous chloride, $SnCl_2$. Pass some of the gas from the generator into each tube. Sulphides of the metals are formed; note the color of each precipitate and write the equations which represent the reactions that take place.

(d) Repeat (c) using, instead of the gas, water through which the gas has been passed. What is the result?

(e) Hydrogen sulphide is thus used in analytical operations, and is a group reagent. Pass some of the gas, or pour some of the solution used in (d) into 5^{cc} of a solution of barium nitrate. Is a precipitate formed? Mix 5^{cc} of the lead nitrate solution with 5^{cc} of the barium nitrate solution in a test tube, and pass the gas into the liquid. What is precipitated? How could you separate the lead from the barium?

(f) Pour a little lead acetate solution on a piece of filter paper and allow the gas to come in contact with it, or pour a little of the water solution over it. Note the change. What is formed? This is a characteristic test.

SULPHURIC ACID.

32. This experiment should be performed with the assistance of the teacher as it requires careful manipulation.

(a) Take a large flask and insert a stopper having five openings. Pass a delivery tube from three of these openings to three smaller flasks, and leave the others open to the air. It is advisable, when convenient, to force air into the large flask through one of the openings by means of a pair of bellows. Into one of the small flasks put some copper turnings, or foil, and concentrated sulphuric acid; into another copper turnings or foil and dilute nitric acid; into the third water. Heat the flasks containing water, and sulphuric acid and copper. Notice the fumes that pass into the large flask. A current of steam is formed; sulphur dioxide; and oxides of nitrogen—mainly nitric oxide. These gases react upon one another in contact with the air and form sulphuric acid.

This experiment may be performed on a still smaller scale by using test tubes instead of flasks.

(b) 1. Test the liquid formed with red and blue litmus paper. 2. Pour 15^{cc} of water into an evaporating dish and add 5^{cc} of concentrated sulphuric acid. What is the effect upon the temperature of the solution? Save the dilute acid. 3. Take 5^{cc} of the dilute acid in a test tube and add barium chloride solution, $BaCl_2$. What is the color of the precipitate formed? What is it? Write the equation. This is the characteristic test for sulphuric acid and soluble sulphates. Try the solubility of the precipitate in acids.

4. Put some wood shavings into an evaporating dish and pour over them some concentrated sulphuric acid.

Note the effect. How does the product compare with the charcoal formed in (b), Exp. 24? Is there any analogy between the two methods? Which is the ordinary method of preparation?

ACIDS, BASES, SALTS, ETC.

Acids consist of hydrogen with a negative element; i. e., a non-metal, (Hydracids; as hydrochloric, HCl, and hydrogen sulphide, H_2S), or with oxygen and a negative element (Oxyacids, as nitric, HNO_3, and sulphuric, H_2SO_4). Thio-acids contain sulphur in place of oxygen. Acids generally redden litmus, especially those which are soluble—all the stronger acids are soluble. Anhydrides are oxyacids minus water. Mono- di- tri- and tetrabasic acids contain one, two, three, and four atoms of basic or replaceable hydrogen to the molecule; as, HCl, H_2SO_4, H_3PO_4, H_4SiO_4.

Elements which combine with hydrogen or hydrogen and oxygen to form compounds with acid properties are called acid-forming elements or non-metals; such as sulphur, nitrogen, fluorine, chlorine, bromine, iodine, phosphorus, arsenic, carbon, and silicon.

Metals are those elements which combine with oxygen, or with oxygen and hydrogen, to form compounds which have basic properties. They are called base-forming elements or metals; such as potassium, sodium, calcium, magnesium, aluminum, zinc, iron, lead, tin, copper, silver, mercury, platinum, and gold.

Bases (hydroxides or hydrates) contain a metal or positive element with hydrogen and oxygen. The strongest bases are the Caustic Alkalis, and the Alkaline Earths. The Caustic Alkalis, potassium hydroxide, KOH; sodium hydroxide, NaOH; and ammonium-hydroxide, NH_4OH, are very soluble in water, and their solutions turn litmus blue. The Alkaline Earths, barium hydroxide, $Ba(OH)_2$; strontium hydroxide, $Sr(OH)_2$; and Calcium Hydroxide, $Ca(OH)_2$, are less soluble but turn litmus blue. Most other bases are insoluble in water and do not turn litmus blue.

The substances formed when an acid neutralizes a base are called salts. Water is formed at the same time. Besides litmus, other indicators, chiefly organic, as cochineal, methyl orange, etc., may be used to distinguish acids from alkalies by change of color. The salts formed by neutralizing sulphuric acid are called sulphates; those formed from nitric acid are called nitrates; and those derived from hydrochloric acid are called chlorides.

A normal salt is one which is formed by replacing all the hydrogen of an acid with a metal; as sodium carbonate, Na_2CO_3; zinc sulphate, $ZnSO_4$. An acid salt is one which is formed by replacing only a part of the hydrogen of an acid with a metal, as $KHSO_4$, and $NaHCO_3$. A basic salt is one in which all the hydrogen is replaced by a metal and a further quantity of oxide or hydrate enters into the molecule, as $ZnSO_4 . ZnO$.

33. (a) Evaporate to dryness in a porcelain evaporating dish, 10^{cc} of dilute hydrochloric acid, note the appearance and amount of residue.

(b) Repeat (a) with 10^{cc} sodium hydrate solution, NaOH.

(c) Take 10 to 15^{cc} of dilute hydrochloric acid in an evaporating dish, add sodium hydrate drop by drop till the solution no longer affects either red or blue litmus. Test by inserting small bits of litmus paper, or put one or two drops of litmus solution into the liquid. Evaporate to dryness, cool, and examine the residue. What does it taste like? Dissolve a little in water.

Does it affect litmus? Write the equation which shows what has taken place.

(d) Repeat (c) using sulphuric acid and sodium hydrate.

(e) Repeat (c) using nitric acid and potassium hydrate.

NEUTRALIZATION.

34. (a) Fasten two burettes to a ring-stand. Fill one with sulphuric acid, the other with prepared sodium hydrate containing .05 grams of actual sodium hydrate to the cubic centimeter. (Ask for the liquids to be used.) In using burettes, if previously used for solutions of different strength or composition, or if not perfectly dry and clean, rinse well with water, and then with a small quantity of the liquid to be used. Always fill with a clean dry funnel. Read the level carefully by the lower meniscus, before and after drawing out the liquid.

(b) Run about 10^{cc} of the soda solution, noting the exact amount, into a clean beaker standing on white paper; add two or three drops of litmus solution for an indicator, then run in acid little by little, stirring constantly, till neutral; the slightest excess of acid is indicated by a faint permanent pink color. Note the exact volume of each liquid taken and then determine the ratio—1:X.

Form of Noting Burette Readings:

Alkali (NaOH)	Acid (H_2SO_4)
2.6	0.
12.8	15.5

Volume 10.2 : 15.5=1:X. X=1.5+

(c) Rinse the beaker and redetermine with a somewhat larger quantity of sodium hydrate.

(d) Take about 15^{cc} of the acid solution in a clean beaker, add the indicator, and then run in the soda solution till neutral (end of reaction is disappearance of pink color). Compare the value of X found, and take the mean of the two most concordant as the true value of X. What does the experiment show regarding combination in definite proportions? Write reactions corresponding to what has taken place. As one cubic centimeter of sodium hydrate is known to contain .05 grams of sodium hydrate, calculate: How many grams of sulphuric acid will neutralize 1^{cc} of the sodium hydrate. How many grams of sulphuric acid there are in 1^{cc} of the sulphuric acid solution. By this last calculation you will standardize the acid solution. Use this standard to determine by a similar procedure:

(e) What weight of potassium hydrate there is in the total amount of test solution given you by your instructor.

Acidimetry and Alkalimetry are based on these methods of neutralization (saturation); a known quantity of pure acid or pure alkali being taken as a starting-point.

Problem: — Write the equation and calculate how many grams of actual sulphuric acid are needed to neutralize 5 grams of actual sodium hydrate. How much sodium sulphate will be formed?

PART II.

THE METALS AND THEIR COMPOUNDS.

POTASSIUM.

35. (a) (Always handle potassium and sodium with forceps.)

Cut off a small piece of potassium from one of the sticks in the bottle, and note the appearance of the cut portion. Place the piece of potassium on your ring-stand and leave exposed to the air. Note the changes it undergoes.

(b) Take a small piece of potassium, about one-fourth the size of a pea, from the bottle; and, after absorbing the adhering oil with a filter paper, drop it upon the surface of water in an evaporating dish. Is potassium heavier or lighter than water? Why is potassium kept under oil? Drop a second piece of potassium upon the water and look at the flame through a blue glass. What is the color of the flame as seen through the glass?

(c) Examine the water in the evaporating dish; wet the fingers with it; try its action on red litmus paper. Write the equation which represents the reaction that has taken place.

(d) Some volatile substances produce characteristic colors. It is necessary to moisten some with hydrochloric acid or concentrated sulphuric acid. Put some fine potassium chloride in a watch crystal and moisten with hydrochloric acid. Make a loop in the end of a piece of platinum wire, and dip it into the potassium chloride. Hold it in the outer edge of a Bunsen or alcohol flame and observe the color of the flame.

(e) Repeat the flame test using another potassium salt. Look at the flame through a blue glass. What is its appearance? In most cases the platinum wire may be dipped into strong solutions of the salt, or the wire moistened and dipped into a little of the salt.

POTASSIUM COMPOUNDS.

36. (a) The Hydroxide.

Dissolve 10 grams of potassium carbonate in about 125^{cc} of water and boil in an iron (or silver) dish. Why? Slowly add 5 grams of slaked lime to the boiling liquid, and stir constantly until all the lime has been added. Allow the solution to cool and then decant off the clear liquid into a bottle and use when required. Try its action upon litmus paper. In what other way has potassium hydrate been prepared?

(b) How may potassium sulphate, and potassium nitrate (saltpetre) be made? Review Experiment 33.

Most of the potassium nitrate in use is made from sodium nitrate (chili saltpetre) by treating with potassium chloride. Write the equation.

Saltpetre or nitre is used in the preparation of sulphuric acid (For what purpose?), and in the preparation of gunpowder.

(c) Gunpowder.

Mix together intimately in a mortar about 4 grams of potassium nitrate; and one gram of charcoal and sulphur, using a little more charcoal than sulphur. Pour the powder on the iron base of your ring-stand and set fire to it. Potassium nitrate is easily broken up and contains enough oxygen for the combustion of the mass. Gases, principally carbon dioxide and nitrogen, are liberated; and, at the time of combustion, occupy several hundred times the volume of the solid powder. Hence the great explosive force when the powder is confined.

(d) Colored flame.

Mix intimately in a mortar 2 grams of powdered strontium nitrate; 2 grams of powdered potassium chlorate; and one-half gram of flowers of sulphur. Set fire to the mixture as before. What is the color of the flame?

(e) Repeat the same experiment using barium nitrate instead of strontium nitrate. What is the color of the flame produced?

SODIUM.

37. (a) Examine a piece of metallic sodium, and leave it exposed to the air as in the case of potassium.

(b) Throw a piece of sodium upon the surface of water; and when it has disappeared, throw a second piece upon the water and touch it with a lighted match. The same effect may be produced by throwing the sodium upon hot water. Try it. How does the action of sodium upon water differ from the action of potassium upon water?

(c) Repeat (d) and (e) Experiment 35, using sodium salts instead of potassium salts. What is the color of the flame? What effect has the blue glass?

(d) Try a mixture of a sodium salt and a potassium salt. What is the color of the flame? Could you detect the presence of potassium in the mixture by looking at the flame?

Look at the flame through the blue glass. What is the appearance of the flame? How could you distinguish between potassium and sodium compounds?

(e) Examine a number of sodium compounds as to color and solubility in water.

(f) Compare briefly the properties of potassium and its compounds with the properties of sodium and its compounds.

SODIUM COMPOUNDS.

38. (a) How may the following sodium compounds be prepared? Sodium chloride, sodium sulphate, and sodium nitrate. See Exp. 33. Sodium chloride is obtained in large quantities from sea water. How? The preparation of sodium hydroxide is similar to that of potassium hydroxide. Write the equation.

(b) Sodium carbonate. (Solvay or ammonia process.)

Take about 25^{cc} of ammonia solution and pass carbon dioxide from a generator into it until the carbon dioxide is no longer absorbed. A solution of acid ammonium carbonate is formed.

$NH_4OH + CO_2 = HNH_4CO_3$.

Slowly add to this a strong solution of sodium chloride as long as a precipitate is formed. This is monosodium carbonate, which is comparatively difficultly soluble in water.

$HNH_4CO_3 + NaCl = HNaCO_3 + NH_4Cl$.

What is left in solution?

Filter the precipitate and dry in an oven. (It may be partially dried by pressing between filter papers.)

Transfer the precipitate to a crucible or ignition tube, and heat until carbon dioxide is no longer given off. The residue is sodium carbonate.

$2HNaCO_3 = Na_2CO_3 + CO_2 + H_2O$.

Put some of the residue in a test tube and add a little

dilute hydrochloric acid. What is given off? Determine the presence of the metal by the flame test. What is the color of the flame?

AMMONIUM COMPOUNDS.

39. (a) Ammonium is a hypothetical metal, being too unstable to exist alone.

Review the experiments on ammonia. What does ammonia gas dissolved in water form? How does it affect litmus paper? Name a characteristic test for ammonia. See (a) Experiment 18.

(b) Examine a number of the compounds of ammonium as to color and solubility in water. How do they compare with potassium and sodium compounds in these respects? Do ammonium salts give a characteristic flame.

Always have your platinum wire clean before trying the flame test. Clean the wire by dipping it into hydrochloric acid and igniting. Sometimes it is necessary to scrape the wire slightly with a knife.

(c) Ammonium sulphide.

Take 50^{cc} of a comparatively strong solution of ammonia, and divide it into two parts of about 25^{cc} each. Pass hydrogen sulphide from a generator into one part until the solution is saturated. A characteristic odor will be noted when the solution is near saturation.

The product is a solution of ammonium hydrosulphide. Add to this the other part of the ammonia solution and ammonium sulphide will be formed. Note the odor and color of the liquid. Pour it into a bottle and cork securely.

Ammonium sulphide is a group reagent and is used to precipitate those sulphides which are soluble in dilute hydrochloric acid. Take two test tubes containing two or three cubic centimeters of zinc sulphate solution. Pour a little hydrochloric acid into each test tube. Is a precipitate formed?

Add a few drops of hydrogen sulphide solution to one and a few drops of ammonium sulphide to the other. What are the results?

Repeat the tests using cobaltous chloride instead of zinc sulphate.

(d) How are the following compounds formed:—

Ammonium chloride, ammonium nitrate, and ammonium sulphate?

Write the equations.

CALCIUM COMPOUNDS.

40. The element, calcium, is not found uncombined. It has no practical application, hence it is not made in any considerable quantity.

(a) Calcium Hydrate.

Put 10 grams of quicklime (calcium oxide) in an evaporating dish and slowly add about 20^{cc} of water to it. Observe what takes place. Slaked lime (calcium hydrate) is formed, and the process is called slaking.

Add 300 or 400^{cc} of water to the slaked lime and pour the whole into a bottle and cork securely. Examine it the next laboratory hour. Has any of the lime dissolved? Test some of the clear solution with litmus paper. Is there any change? The solution is known as lime-water. It may be poured from your bottle into the bottle labeled "Lime-water."

What takes place when you blow your breath through clear lime-water? What change does it undergo when exposed to the air? Review (a) and (f) Experiment 26.

Add lime-water to a solution of ferric chloride. Ferric hydroxide is thrown down. What is its color?

Add a little sulphuric acid to lime-water. What is formed?

(b) Calcium sulphate (gypsum).

Heat some powdered gypsum in an ignition tube. Does it contain water of crystallization?

Put 4 or 5 grams of gypsum in a crucible and heat for twenty or thirty minutes in an air bath or over a flame at about 150°—avoid heating above 200°.

Add enough water to the residue to form a paste and allow it to stand. Moisten some gypsum that has not been heated and allow it to stand for a time. Is there any difference between the two? Gypsum heated in this way forms a powder known as plaster of Paris.

(c) Take the carbonate, the chloride, and the sulphate of calcium and try their solubility in water, in acids (hydrochloric and nitric), and in alcohol.

What has calcium chloride been used for in previous experiments? Water containing calcium carbonate, or water containing calcium sulphate in solution, is called a hard water. The former, temporarily hard because the hardness is easily removed by boiling; the latter, permanently hard because the hardness is not removed by boiling.

(d) Take a little calcium chloride and see what color it gives to the flame. Compare it with sodium.

What tests would you employ to distinguish between the chlorides of potassium, sodium, ammonium, and calcium?

ZINC.

41. (a) Examine some metallic zinc. What is its color? What effect has the common acids (hydrochloric,

sulphuric and nitric) upon ordinary zinc? What gas is usually evolved?

Try the effect of caustic alkalies upon zinc. See if you can write the equations expressing the reactions.

For what purpose has zinc been previously used? Mention any uses of zinc with which you are familiar.

What is the equivalent weight of zinc?

(b) Heat a small piece of zinc on charcoal in the reducing flame. Does the zinc burn? What is the residue formed?

Note the color of the sublimate while hot and when cold? When it becomes cool moisten with dilute cobalt nitrate and heat again. What is the color of the sublimate?

ZINC COMPOUNDS.

42. (a) Examine several of the compounds of zinc. What is their usual color?

(b) Take four test tubes and pour into each about 5^{cc} of zinc sulphate solution. Add to one of these a solution of potassium hydroxide; to another, a solution of sodium carbonate; to the third, ammonium hydrate solution; and to the fourth, a solution of ammonium sulphide. Give the colors of the precipitates. Write the equations to show what is formed in each case. Underline the parts which represent the precipitates.

(c) Take the test tube in which you added potassium hydroxide, and add an excess of the reagent. What is the effect? Divide the solution into two parts. Dilute one part, and boil the other. What are the results?

OXIDATION AND REDUCTION.

Oxidation takes place when oxygen or any negative element or group is added to an element or compound, and when hydrogen or any positive element or group is removed—it consists in the increase of the proportion of the more negative constituents.

Reduction takes place when oxygen or any negative element or group is removed from a compound, or when hydrogen or any positive element or group is added—it is the reverse of oxidation.

The valence of an element (monad, dyad, triad, etc.) is the number of bonds or units of chemical force it possesses. It is measured by the number of atoms of hydrogen or chlorine which one of its atoms combines with or replaces. Oxidation or reduction takes place when the number of acting bonds of an atom of any element suffers change.

The following are the principal elements which form two series of salts: — Iron, mercury, tin, antimony, arsenic, manganese, and copper. By suitable means, the lower (ous) salts of each can be converted into the higher (ic) salts and vice versa.

In the following experiments on oxidation and reduction, use very small quantities of the substances called for, and have the vessels you use well cleaned. Notice carefully the nature of each reaction.

43. (a) Burn a little sulphur in air. What is formed? Has oxidation or reduction taken place?

(b) Put a little finely powdered sulphur in a test tube and add about 5^{cc} of nitric acid. Warm for about ten minutes. Part of the sulphur is oxidized to SO_3.

$$S + 2HNO_3 = H_2SO_4 + 2NO.$$

Test the presence of sulphuric acid by diluting the solution to four or five volumes and adding barium chloride. A white precipitate, insoluble in acids, indicates a sulphate. Write the equation.

(c) Place a drop or two of mercuric chloride solution on a clean piece of copper or zinc. It is reduced finally to metallic mercury. Write the equation. What is the nature of the change in the nitric acid in (b), and of the zinc or copper in (c)?

(d) Take 5^{cc} of mercuric chloride, $HgCl_2$, in a test tube, and add one or two drops of stannous chloride, $SnCl_2$; warm and note the result. Now add a considerable amount of stannous chloride, heat and observe the result as before. Stannic chloride, $SnCl_4$, is formed in each case; in the first mercurous chloride, Hg_2Cl_2, and in the second mercury is precipitated.

(1) $2HgCl_2 + SnCl_2 = Hg_2Cl_2 + SnCl_4$.
(2) $HgCl_2 + SnCl_2 = Hg + SnCl_4$.

(e) Put a small globule of mercury in a test tube, and add 5^{cc} of dilute (diluted 5 to 1) nitric acid. Warm very gently for a few minutes, if necessary to produce action. Mercurous nitrate is formed. Test the liquid with a few drops of hydrochloric acid. What is the color of the precipitate formed? What does it indicate? Write the equation.

When hot concentrated nitric acid is used in excess, mercuric nitrate is formed which gives no precipitate when treated with hydrochloric acid. Mercuric chloride is soluble.

Iodine as a Test for Oxidizing and Reducing Agents.

The liberation of iodine from potassium iodide or hydriodic acid indicates an oxidizing agent, the free iodine is recognized by the brown color it gives to water; and the wine color it gives to kerosene, carbon bisulphide, etc. The test can be made more delicate by introducing freshly prepared starch paste which is colored blue by a mere trace of free iodine. (The color of the iodide of starch disappears temporarily while heated.)

Conversely, the removal of this blue color generally indicates a reducing agent.

44.. (a) Dissolve a small crystal of potassium iodide in about 25^{cc} of water, or take 5^{cc} of the prepared potassium iodide solution and dilute it.

Put 3 or 4^{cc} of the solution into each of three test tubes, and add to each about 2^{cc} of kerosene or a few drops of carbon bisulphide. Into one test tube add a small quantity of ferric chloride solution; into another, a little copper sulphate solution; and into the third, dilute nitric acid. Observe any changes in appearance.

(1) $Fe_2Cl_6 + 2KI = I_2 + 2KCl + 2FeCl_2$.
(2) $2CuSO_4 + 4KI = I_2 + 2K_2SO_4 + Cu_2I_2$.
(3) $4HNO_3 + 3KI = I_3 + 3KNO_3 + NO + 2H_2O$.

(b) Prepare some starch paste and add some potassium iodide solution to it; stir well and keep covered. Take small quantities in test tubes and add mere traces of the following:

(1) Ferric chloride, (2) copper sulphate, (3) mercuric chloride, (4) chlorine water, (add this reagent drop by drop and finally in considerable quantity). What changes do you notice?

Heat some of the solutions and then allow them to cool. What is the effect?

$HgCl_2 + 2KI = 2KCl + HgI_2$.

$Cl + KI = KCl + I$ (with comparatively little chlorine).

(c) Make some of the starch paste, containing potassium iodide, blue by adding a drop or two of bromine or chlorine water.

To small quantities of this in three test tubes, add solutions of the following:

(1) Hydrogen sulphide, (2) stannous chloride, (3) sodium hydrate. Is there any change in color produced?
(1) $H_2S + 2I = 2HI + S$.
(2) $2SnCl_2 + 4I = SnCl_4 + SnI_4$.
(3) $6NaOH + 6I = 3H_2O + 5NaI + NaIO_3$.

IRON.

45. (a) What is the color of a freshly broken piece of iron? What is "iron rust"?

Heat a little ferric chloride (or any iron compound) on charcoal. What is the color of the residue? Allow it to cool and test with a magnet. Has it magnetic properties? Try another compound.

Examine several of the ferric and the ferrous salts and solutions. Can you make any distinction as to color?

IRON COMPOUNDS (OXIDATION AND REDUCTION).

46. (a) Place about one-half gram of fine iron wire or filings in a small flask and add about 50^{cc} of dilute sulphuric acid, and then a little sodium carbonate. (Carbon dioxide forms and expels the air.) Insert a delivery tube and warm gently till action ceases.

Carbon, silicon, etc., remain undissolved. What is in solution?

Write the equation representing the action of sulphuric acid on iron.

Allow the undissolved portion to settle, and then pour off the clear solution—one-half into a beaker, the other half into a bottle. Dilute the solution in the bottle by adding an equal volume of water; add a pinch of sodium carbonate to displace the air, and when action ceases, cork the bottle.

Heat the ferrous sulphate in the beaker to boiling and add 4 or 5^{cc} of concentrated nitric acid and evaporate to one-half. If necessary, add more nitric acid and boil again until you notice a distinct change in color. Ferric sulphate is formed. Observe the characteristic colors of ferrous and ferric solutions.

(b) Take about a cubic centimeter of the ferrous sulphate solution and add at once a solution of sodium hydroxide; ferrous hydroxide is precipitated.

Treat a similar amount of ferric sulphate with the sodium hydroxide solution; ferric hydroxide is precipitated. What is the appearance of each precipitate? Write the equation expressing the reaction in each case.

Pour a little of the ferrous sulphate solution into a test tube and leave it, and also the test tube containing the ferrous hydroxide, open to the air. Shake them from time to time. Do you notice any change? What forms in each case?

(c) 1. Treat a small quantity of ferric sulphate with about 10^{cc} of hydrogen sulphide solution; warm slightly. $Fe_2(SO_4)_3 + H_2S = 2FeSO_4 + H_2SO_4 + S.$ (white precipitate).

2. Place a piece of zinc in a little of the ferric sulphate solution and leave for ten minutes. What change do you notice? Write the equation expressing the reaction.

Mention several oxidizing agents, and several reducing agents.

COPPER.

47. (a) Examine some copper wire or sheet copper; also examine some of the metallic copper in the stoppered bottle. Is there any difference in appearance between that in the bottle and that exposed to the moist air of the room?

Mention any uses of copper with which you are familiar.

Test the effect of the common acids, both the concentrated and the dilute, upon metallic copper. Does heat modify the action?

(b) Examine several of the compounds of copper. Which compound have you already examined, and for what purpose?

What seems to be the general color of the solutions of the copper compounds? Take a copper compound, moisten a little with hydrochloric acid, and see what color it gives to flames.

Test some of the solutions to see if they have either an acid or an alkaline reaction.

(c) How is copper sulphate made? Obtain some of the solution and pour about 5^{cc} into each of three test tubes; then try the effect of each of the following solutions: Potassium hydroxide, hydrogen sulphide, and potassium ferrocyanide. Give the color of each precipitate. Write the equations and underline the parts representing the precipitates.

Heat the test tube into which potassium hydroxide was added. Copper oxide is formed. What is its color? write the equation.

EQUIVALENT WEIGHT OF COPPER.

48. (a) Brighten some narrow strips of pure zinc, and weigh out exactly one gram. Clean thoroughly a comparatively large evaporating dish and place the zinc strips, loosely coiled, in the bottom. Weigh on a rough balance some copper sulphate crystals, about ten times the weight of zinc taken, dissolve in about 100^{cc} of hot water, and then filter the hot solution upon the zinc in the basin. Place the dish on your ring-stand on a wire gauze and heat from one to two hours (or, if more convenient, allow it to remain covered till the next laboratory period.) until the deposit ceases to increase.

(b) Allow the deposit to settle, and then decant off all the liquid possible through a filter paper into a large beaker. Add water to the basin, heat, allow the copper to settle, and decant as before. Wash the copper several times in this manner until a portion of the wash water in a test tube gives no turbidity when barium chloride is added. Finally transfer the copper deposit to the filter, wash again to settle it, and dry in an oven at a temperature not above $100°$.

(c) Carefully transfer the metallic copper to a watch glass and weigh accurately. This amount of copper has been replaced by one gram of zinc. Hence, knowing the equivalent of zinc from Experiment 15, calculate the equivalent weight of copper.

Copper may also be precipitated from its salts by iron and some other metals. Hence their equivalent weight may be determined in a similar manner.

LEAD.

49. (a) Take a piece of metallic lead and scrape off the outer surface with a knife. What is its color?

What is the appearance of lead that has been exposed to the air for some time? See if you can write on paper with the metal. Will the common acids dissolve lead? Try them.

(b) Place on a piece of charcoal a little lead sulphide (galena). Cover it with sodium carbonate and heat in the reducing flame. Note the color of the sublimate while hot and when cold. Is it volatile? Remove the beads of metal and test properties. Can you mark on paper with them?

(c) 1. Place in a test tube a piece of bright sheet zinc and pour over it 5 or 10^{cc} of lead acetate solution. Set the tube to one side and leave undisturbed for some time. Explain the action that has taken place. Write the equation.

2. Remove the zinc, wash thoroughly, and scrape the deposit off into a test tube. Pour enough dilute nitric acid into the test tube to cover the lead deposit. Warm slightly and as soon as action ceases, dilute to about 10^{cc}.

3. Divide the solution into four parts. To one part, add hydrogen sulphide solution; to another, sulphuric acid; to the third, potassium chromate; and to the fourth, hydrochloric acid. What is the color of the sulphide? the sulphate? the chromate? and the chloride? Write the equations expressing the reactions.

4 Divide the chloride into two parts, and test the solubility in cold water and in hot water. Is it soluble?

Divide the hot solution into two parts. Allow one part to cool, and add potassium bichromate solution to the other. What are the results?

SILVER.

50. (a) Dissolve half of a silver dime in a little dilute nitric acid in a beaker. Warm gently till action is over, then evaporate nearly to dryness and dilute with 100^{cc} of water.

The solution contains silver nitrate, copper nitrate, and nitric acid. (Traces of gold are sometimes found in the form of little black specks. These may be separated from the solution by filtering.) Which of the compounds gives the solution its color?

All United States silver coins are alloyed with about 10 per cent. of copper.

Heat the solution to boiling, add hydrochloric acid slowly, and stir till the precipitate gathers in a lump. What is the color of the precipitate? What is it? What remains in solution? Filter out the precipitate and dry in an air bath heated to 100°–110°. When the precipitate is dry, mix a little sodium carbonate with it, and heat on charcoal in the reducing flame of the blowpipe. White beads of metallic silver are formed. Remove these carefully from the charcoal and place them in an evaporating dish. Dissolve in a little dilute nitric acid and evaporate to dryness in a water bath. What is formed? Dissolve the residue in water and filter into a bottle of dark colored glass, or a bottle covered with dark paper.

(b) Pour about one-half cubic centimeter of the clear silver nitrate solution into each of three test tubes, and add 5^{cc} of water to each. Now add sodium chloride solution to one, potassium bromide solution to another, and potassium iodide solution to the third. Name each precipitate and give its color?

Expose all to the light and watch closely for any changes.

Silver salts are used extensively in photography on account of the change produced by light.

51. (a) Place in a test tube a strip of metallic zinc and pour over it 3 or 4^{cc} of the silver nitrate solution prepared in Experiment 50. Let it stand for some time without disturbing. Remove the strip from the tube and wash thoroughly with water. What is the appearance of the deposit? Scrape it off and dissolve in dilute nitric acid.

(b) Divide the solution into two parts and dilute each with about 5^{cc} of water.

Add a few drops of hydrochloric acid to one part. How does the precipitate compare with the precipitate formed in (a) Exp. 50? Divide the precipitate into three parts and test its solubility in hot water, nitric acid and in ammonium hydroxide. Compare with lead chloride, (c) 4, Experiment 49.

(c) Take the other part of the silver solution retained from (b), and add a little hydrogen sulphide solution. What is the color of the precipitate? What is it?

Divide the precipitate into three parts. Add cold nitric acid to one part, hot nitric acid to another, and potassium cyanide to the third part. Note results.

MERCURY.

52. (a) In what form is metallic mercury? Can you mention any other element that is usually in the same form? What is the appearance of mercury?

(b) Take four test tubes: put a piece of zinc into one, a piece of iron into another, a piece of copper into a third, and a piece of tin into the fourth. Cover each metal with a solution of mercurous nitrate. After a few minutes, remove the metals and examine. Rub each with a piece of soft cloth. Are all permanently affected?

Drop a globule of metallic mercury upon a piece of sheet zinc and rub it with a cloth. Do you obtain the same result as with the piece of zinc previously used?

What are alloys of mercury with other metals called?

(c) Heat a little mercuric oxide in a closed tube. What change in appearance do you notice? Explain the change.

For what purpose has mercuric oxide been used before?

(d) Mix some mercurous chloride (calomel) with a little sodium carbonate and heat in a closed tube Is the compound reduced to the metal?

(e) Put a globule of mercury in a test tube and dissolve in nitric acid. Dilute and then add a few drops of hydrochloric acid to the solution. What is the color of the precipitate? What is it?

Divide the precipitate into two parts: add a little ammonium hydroxide to one part. What is the effect? Add water to the other part and boil it. Compare with the solubility of lead chloride and silver chloride in water. (c) 4. Exp. 49, and (b) Exp. 51.

How could you separate lead nitrate, silver nitrate, and mercurous nitrate from one another?

Hydrochloric acid gives no precipitate when added to mercuric solutions.

ACTION OF ACIDS ON THE METALS.

53. (a) In every case brighten metals used by filing or with sand paper.

Put into a test tube 2^{cc} of dilute sulphuric acid and insert a small piece of zinc. Note the action. Warm (not boil) the acid—is the action modified? Add more zinc and continue heating; can action be carried on indefinitely?

(b) Take two test tubes each containing about 5^{cc} of dilute sulphuric acid. Put a piece of smooth zinc into each, warm slightly, and note the character of the action.

Drop on the zinc in one tube a piece of platinum or copper wire, or a silver coin; in the other tube put a small crystal (or two or three drops of a solution) of copper sulphate. Is action more, or less, energetic?

(c) Cut a long, narrow strip of zinc, about 10^{cm}

by 3^{mm}, and place it in a test tube. Add enough dilute sulphuric acid to half cover the zinc; warm gently.

At what part of the liquid is the action most energetic?

(d) Take two pieces of zinc of equal size and equal thickness (about 3^{cm} by 3^{mm}), and fold one up closely several times.

Place both in dilute sulphuric, or hydrochloric, acid and observe which dissolves first. Expain.

(e) Take two *small* pinches of about equal size of iron filings; place in test tubes and add to each about 5^{cc} of dilute sulphuric, or hydrochloric, acid. Shake or stir continuously the contents of one tube, letting the other stand in the rack. Which dissolves first? Suggest the cause.

(f) Review your experiments and make a tabulated outline of the action of concentrated, moderately strong (one volume of concentrated acid to one of water), and dilute sulphuric acid; nitric acid; and hydrochloric acid upon the following metals: zinc, iron, copper, lead, and mercury.

Perform tests that have not been previously made, and repeat tests whenever you are in doubt as to the action.

FORMATION OF THE COMPOUNDS OF THE METALS.

A number of the compounds of the metals have already been considered; a few of these, by way of review, and some others will now be studied according to their classification. These will be sufficient to present the general methods of preparation.

CHLORIDES.

54. (a) What compound is formed when zinc is treated with hydrochloric acid? Review (a) Experiment 6.

(b) Review (b) 5, Experiment 23, and state what was formed when you did the experiment.

(c) Add hydrochloric acid to a little quicklime. What takes place? Write the equation.

(d) What takes place when caustic soda is treated with hydrochloric acid? Review (c) Experiment 33.

(e) What is the effect of adding hydrochloric acid to calcium carbonate? See (a) Experiment 26.

As illustrated above, the chlorides are made by treating the metals with chlorine or hydrochloric acid; and by treating an oxide, hydroxide, or carbonate (a salt of a volatile acid) with hydrochloric acid.

(f) Are the chlorides of lead, silver, and mercury soluble, difficultly soluble, or insoluble in water? Review Exps. 49, 51, 52. Test the solubility, in water, of several of the other chlorides of the metals. Are they soluble or insoluble?

If a precipitate is formed when hydrochloric acid is added to a solution, what metal or metals, would you suppose to be present?

OXIDES.

55. (a) Review Experiments 4 and 8, and state how the metals, iron and magnesium, were changed.

(b) What takes place when copper hydrate is heated? Represent the change by an equation. Review (c) Experiment 47.

(c) Put some lead nitrate in an ignition tube and heat. Oxygen and nitrogen peroxide are given off leaving lead oxide behind. What is the appearance of the residue?

(d) When certain carbonates are heated strongly,

carbon dioxide is given off. What is left? How is lime made?

From the above, state how the oxides are made.

HYDROXIDES.

56. (a) How is calcium hydroxide formed? Review (a) Experiment 40.

(b) Put 5^{cc} of magnesium sulphate solution in a test tube and add sodium hydroxide. The precipitate is magnesium hydroxide. What is its appearance? Write the equation representing the reaction. Is the precipitate soluble in hydrochloric acid?

What chlorides are insoluble or difficultly soluble in water?

(c) Add caustic soda solution to a little ferric chloride solution in a test tube. The precipitate is ferric hydroxide. What is its color? Compare with (b) Experiment 46. Would you expect it to be soluble in hydrochloric acid? Why?

Observe that in (b) and (c) a soluble hydroxide has been added to solutions containing metals whose hydroxides are insoluble; hence, the insoluble hydroxides are precipitated.

Name the soluble hydroxides. How is potassium hydroxide made? Do all the hydroxides turn litmus blue?

SULPHIDES.

57. (a) How is ferrous sulphide made? Review (d) Experiment 2. What use have you previously made of ferrous sulphide?

(b) Heat some sulphur to near boiling and introduce into it a piece of bright copper—copper foil or sheet copper. What change takes place? What is the product called?

(c) Put a drop or two of sodium sulphide solution, or hydrogen sulphide solution (any soluble sulphide) on a bright silver coin, and leave for a few minutes. Rinse the coin and examine. How has it changed in appearance? The formation is silver sulphide.

(d) Review (c) Exp. 31, and (c) Exp. 39.

How may the sulphides be made?

What reagent is used to precipitate the sulphides which are soluble in hydrochloric acid?

NITRATES.

58. (a) What is left in solution when a silver coin is dissolved in nitric acid? See (a) Experiment 50.

(b) What is the effect of adding nitric acid to a metal? Review (d) Exp. 21; (c) Exp. 49; and (e) Exp. 52.

(c) What is formed when nitric acid acts upon copper? Review Experiment 20.

Write the equation expressing the reactions which take place when nitric acid is neutralized with ammonium hydroxide, calcium hydroxide, and potassium hydroxide.

(d) Add nitric acid to a little sodium carbonate in a test tube. What is the result?

(e) What is the effect of adding sulphuric acid to sodium nitrate? Review Experiment 21.

Sulphuric acid decomposes all nitrates liberating nitric acid. What gas is given off when a nitrate is heated strongly in a closed tube?

(f) Heat some copper nitrate crystals in a closed tube. Does the salt contain water of crystallization?

(g) Try the solubility, in water, of a number of the nitrates.

SULPHATES.

59. (a) What is the action of sulphuric acid on the metallic hydroxides? What is the color of copper sulphate? Does the removal of the water of crystallization affect the form or color of the crystals? See Experiment 14.

(b) Review the following experiments, and state what sulphates were formed and how: Experiments 6, 15, 21, 22, and 32.

(c) Obtain dilute solutions of lead nitrate, strontium nitrate, and barium chloride; and a strong solution of calcium chloride. The sulphates of lead, strontium, and barium are insoluble in water; the sulphate of calcium difficultly soluble. Hence a precipitate is formed when sulphuric acid is added to solutions of these metals.

Add sulphuric acid to the solutions, and note the color of each precipitate.

(d) The same insoluble sulphates may be formed by adding any soluble sulphate to the solutions.

Obtain a number of the sulphates from the shelf and test their solubility in water. Then take samples of the solutions named in (c) and form the sulphates by adding soluble sulphates. What is the characteristic test for soluble sulphates?

(e) Heat some iron sulphate on charcoal in the reducing flame. Note the odor of the gas given off. What is it? Sulphates of all the heavy metals give off the same gas.

CARBONATES.

60. (a) Review Experiment 26. What carbonates were formed and how? How is sodium carbonate made?

(b) Test the solubility, in water, of the carbonates

of potassium, sodium, and ammonium. What is the effect of boiling the solutions?

(c) Test the solubility, in water, of other carbonates.

(d) Obtain solutions of the following compounds: Lead nitrate, iron sulphate, copper sulphate, barium chloride, and calcium chloride. Add to each a little of a solution of a soluble carbonate. Precipitates (carbonates of the metals) will be formed in the solution of all the salts of the metals whose carbonates are insoluble in water.

How do the results compare with the tests made in (c)?

Filter off the precipitates in each case, wash, and test for carbonates with acids. What gas is given off?

(e) What is usually the effect of heating a carbonate strongly? Review Experiment 55.

CRYSTALLIZATION.

"Crystals are solids bounded by plane faces inclined at definite angles." While there are a great number of forms of crystals, it has been found that every form can be referred to one or other of six systems. But crystals of the same form may differ widely in appearance and habit; for example, the faces may be unequally developed, but he angles remain constant. A given chemical compound usually crystallizes, under the same conditions, in the same form. The form, "habit," and optical properties of a crystal serve as a guide to its composition.

Crystallization can only take place when the particles or molecules are free to arrange themselves. The most slowly formed crystals are, as a rule, the largest and most perfect.

61. (a) Carefully clean and dry some glass plates and put on them, by means of a glass rod or pipette, a large drop of each of the solutions named and in the order given. Use saturated solutions. Sodium chloride, potassium bromide, sodium nitrate, potassium nitrate, potassium chlorate, mercuric chloride, ammonium chloride, copper sulphate, ferrous sulphate, zinc sulphate, potash alum, ammonium alum, chrome alum, sulphur (in carbon bisulphide). Leave two or three hours and then examine with a lens. Note the appearance and resemblance of crystals of certain salts.

Crystals of salts of similar molecular structure often occur in the same or very similar forms. Such crystals are said to be isomorphous; thus, all the alums crystallize in octahedra; so also sodium chloride, potassium chloride, potassium bromide, and potassium iodide all crystallize in cubes.

The same substance may, under different conditions, crystallize in two or more distinct forms,—e. g. sulphur (see Exp. 29.) and zinc sulphate. Such substances are said to be dimorphous.

Water of crystallization is essential to the form of some crystals, and in many cases to the color (see Exp. 59), while other crystals contain none. (See Experiment 12.)

Crystals may be obtained from the gaseous state in the case of those substances which do not liquefy before solidifying.

(b) Put a small piece of iodine in a watch glass and place over it a glass plate; warm the lower glass very gently.

Notice the iodine crystals formed on the glass plate.

From a mixed solution certain salts will crystallize out together as a double salt, which is not a mere mixture, as the number of molecules bear a definite ratio; thus a solution of the sulphates of aluminum and potassium yield, upon evaporation, crystals of alum of the composition $K_2SO_4 \cdot Al_2(SO_4)_3 \cdot 24H_2O$.

Note —A solution should be prepared, concentrated, and poured into a shallow crystallizing dish so that the class may observe the growth of the crystals from day to day. The temperature must not fluctuate if good crystals are to be had.

Crystals deposited from impure solutions contain less impurity than the solution, i. e. a less proportion; hence crystallizable soluble substances can, by repeated solution and partial recrystallization, be almost absolutely free from all impurities—excepting isomorphous substances, and those salts with which they form double salts.

DETERMINATION OF ATOMIC WEIGHTS

The atoms of most elements in the solid state have approximately the same capacity for heat; as their atomic weights increase, their specific heats decrease, so that the product of the atomic weight times the specific heat approximates to a constant value. The average value is 6.4.

Hence, atomic weight × specific heat = 6.4.

"The equivalent of an element always bears some numerical relation to its atomic weight. As a rule, this relation is a simple one. With hydrogen and chlorine, equivalent and atomic weight are equal; the atomic weight of oxygen is twice its equivalent; while that of nitrogen is three times its equivalent."

Elements whose equivalent and atomic weight are equal are called Monads; those whose atomic weight is twice the equivalet are called Dyads; etc.

"The word Quantivalence or Valency is applied to denote generally the state of an element as regards its function as a monad, dyad, etc."

The valency of an element, then, is expressed by the number of times which the equivalent is contained in the atomic weight.

As the product 6.4 varies somewhat with different metals, the method cannot be used to determine atomic weights exactly, but it decides whether the equivalent, or combining weight, is equal to the atomic weight, or is some fractional proportion of it.

62. (a) Weigh accurately a piece of metallic copper (copper wire loosely coiled if obtainable), and suspend it by a fine wire in a beaker of boiling water.

Counterpoise a calorimeter, and then add somewhat more than enough water to cover the metal,—take a round number of grams (200, 300 or 500) to simplify calculations, and weigh accurately.

In weighing liquids it is best to add a little more than the desired amount and remove the excess by absorbing it with a piece of blotting paper.

Note the exact temperature of the water in the calorimeter. Remove the copper from the boiling water, jerk off as much water as possible, and lower it immediately into the calorimeter. Stir the water with the metal for about a minute. Note the temperature from time to time and take the highest reading.

Calculate from the data obtained the specific heat of copper.

(b) Determine, in a similar manner, the specific heat of tin and of lead.

(c) Having found the specific heats of the metals, calulate from the formula given their respective atomic weights.

Tabulate the values found. Write the names of the metals (copper, tin, and lead, in the order given) in the first column; the corresponding atomic weight in the second; corresponding specific heat in the third; and the product of the atomic weight by the specific heat in the fourth column. Get the average of the three products.

Are the atomic weights of the metals in the order of magnitude, or not? Are the specific heats in the same, or the reverse, order?

How does the atomic weight of copper as determined compare with its equivalent weight found in Experiment 48?

APPENDIX.

TABLE OF COMMON ELEMENTS.

NAME, SYMBOL, AND ATOMIC WEIGHTS IN EVEN NUMBERS.

Aluminum	Al	27	Lead	Pb	205
Antimony	Sb	120	Magnesium	Mg	24
Arsenic	As	74	Manganese	Mn	55
Barium	Ba	136	Mercury	Hg	199
Bismuth	Bi	207	Nickel	Ni	58
Boron	B	11	Nitrogen	N	14
Bromine	Br	80	Oxygen	O	16
Calcium	Ca	40	Phosphorus	P	31
Carbon	C	12	Platinum	Pt	194
Chlorine	Cl	35	Potassium	K	39
Chromium	Cr	52	Silicon	Si	28
Cobalt	Co	59	Silver	Ag	107
Copper	Cu	63	Sodium	Na	23
Fluorine	F	19	Strontium	Sr	87
Gold	Au	196	Sulphur	S	32
Hydrogen	H	1	Tin	Sn	118
Iodine	I	126	Zinc	Zn	65
Iron	Fe	56			

COMPLETE LIST OF CHEMICALS REQUIRED FOR THE COURSE.

ESTIMATE FOR A CLASS OF 12.

Antimony chloride	¼ lb.
Antimony, powdered	¼ lb.
Arsenic chloride	1 oz.
Alcohol	4¾ gal. if used for lamps
Alum, potash	¼ lb.
" chrome	¼ lb.
" ammonium	¼ lb.

Ammonium hydrate, conc.	3	lb.
" nitrate	2	lb.
" sulphate	¼	lb.
" sulphide	¼	lb.
" chloride	½	lb.
" carbonate	1	lb.
Barium chloride	¼	lb.
" nitrate	¼	lb.
Bromine	1	oz.
Boneblack	½	lb.
Borax	¼	lb.
Calcium oxide	2	lb.
" carbonate, lumps	2	lb.
" chloride	½	lb.
" sulphate	¼	lb.
Carbon bisulphide	½	lb.
Cobalt chloride	1	oz.
" nitrate	1	oz.
Copper oxide	1	oz.
" sulphate, pure	½	lb.
" nitrate	¼	lb.
" foil	¼	lb.
" sheet	¼	lb.
" wire	½	lb.
Chlorine water (made in Lab.)		
Cochineal	1	oz.
Charcoal	2 doz.	sticks
Candles	½	dozen
Cotton print	few	pieces
Cardboard	few	pieces
Ether	½	lb.
Ferrous sulphate	½	lb.
" sulphide	2	lb.

EXPERIMENTAL CHEMISTRY

Ferric chloride	3 oz
Filter paper, 5 in. diam	4 packages
Gypsum, powdered	4 oz.
Hydrochloric acid, conc.	6 lb.
Hydrogen sulphide (made in Lab.)	
Iron, sheet	1 lb.
" filings, fine	1 lb.
Iodine	1 oz.
Indigo solution	¼ lb.
Kerosene	1 lb.
Lead nitrate	¼ lb.
" acetate, pure	¼ lb.
" sulphide	¼ lb.
" sheet	½ lb.
Litmus	1 oz.
Litmus paper, red and blue	1 box each
Labels	1 box each of large and small
Magnesium ribbon	¼ oz.
" sulphate	¼ lb.
Manganese dioxide, coarse	2 lb.
Mercury	1 lb.
Mercurous chloride	1 oz.
" nitrate	¼ lb.
Mercuric chloride	¼ lb.
Mercuric oxide	¼ lb.
Nitric acid, conc	6 lb.
Oxalic acid crystals	1 lb.
Oil of turpentine	¼ lb.
Paraffine	1 lb.
Phosphorus	1 oz.
Potassium, metallic	¼ oz.
" hydrate, sticks	1 lb.
" chloride	¼ lb.

Potassium, nitrate		1 lb.
"	carbonate	¼ lb.
"	iodide	¼ lb.
"	bromide	1 oz.
"	cyanide	¼ lb.
"	permanganate	¼ lb.
"	bichromate	¼ lb.
"	chlorate	2 lb.
"	chromate	¼ lb.
"	ferrocyanide	¼ lb.
Platinum foil		2 pieces 1 in. square
"	wire	1 ft.
Silk, unbleached		25 cts
Sodium, metallic		1 oz.
"	chloride, pure	1 lb.
"	sulphide	1 oz.
"	sulphate	¼ lb.
"	hydrate, sticks	1 lb.
"	nitrate	2 lb.
"	carbonate	¼ lb.
Sulphur, roll		½ lb.
"	flowers	½ lb.
Sulphuric acid, conc		9 lb.
Stannous chloride		1 oz.
Starch		½ lb.
Strontium nitrate		¼ lb.
Sugar		1 lb.
Sealing Wax		2 sticks
Tin foil, pure		¼ lb.
Yarn, white woolen		10 cts.
Zinc, granulated		2 lb.
"	sheet	1 lb.
"	sulphate	½ lb.

APPARATUS.

ESTIMATE FOR A CLASS OF TWELVE WITH AN ALLOWANCE FOR SOME BREAKAGE.

12 Asbestos sheets $\frac{1}{8}$ in. thick, 4x4 in.
1 Air-bath (drying oven)
2 Bell jars, $\frac{1}{2}$ gal.
1 Balance, rough.
1 Balance, delicate, with metric weights.
12 Blowpipes, plain with moisture bulb.
2 doz. Beakers, 3 to 7 oz.
2 Burettes 100^{cc} each.
2 pieces Blue Glass, 4x4 in.
1 Barometer.
6 Calcium Chloride U-tubes, plain, 6 in.
10 doz. corks, best quality, Nos. 3 to 10.
2 doz. corks, 1 to 2 in. diameter.
2 Condensers, 18 in. long.
1 doz. Clamps, small.
4 Calorimeters, metal.
3 Crystallizing dishes, 8 in. diam.
10 Deflagrating spoons, $\frac{1}{2}$ in. bowl.
12 Delivery tubes (made by class).
4 Desiccators, 4 in. diam.
1 Electric battery, 2 cells.
1 Electrolysis apparatus, simple form.
2 doz. Evaporating dishes, 2 and 3 oz.
1$\frac{1}{2}$ doz. Flasks, flat bottom, 12 oz.
$\frac{1}{2}$ doz. Flasks, flat bottom 8 oz.
1 doz. Funnels 3$\frac{1}{2}$ in. diam.
2 doz. Funnel tubes, small, 10 in. long.
$\frac{1}{2}$ doz. Files, triangular, 6 in. long.

3 Files, rat tail, 6 in. long.
1 doz. Forceps, common steel, 4 in. long.
2 Graduated cylinders, 50^{cc} and 200^{cc}.
2 Gasoline Lab. lamps, Dangler's. (Not required if gas is used.)
1½ doz. Glass stirring rods, solid glass.
2 lb. Glass tubing, hard and soft, ¼ in. diam.
1 lb. Glass tubing, soft, $\frac{3}{16}$ and $\frac{5}{16}$ in. diam.
4 doz. Glass plates, 3x3 in.
3 nests Hessian crucibles, 4 in nest, small 5s.
½ doz. Iron dishes, 4 in. diam.
2 doz. Ignition tubes, 4 and 6 in. length.
½ doz. Iron water (or gas) pipes 50^{cm} x 2^{cm} diam.
6 Metric rulers.
2 Mortars and pestles, 1 iron 2 pt., 1 porcelain 4½ in. diam.
2 Magnets, horse shoe, 4 in long.
1 Magnifying glass.
¼ doz. Porcelain crucibles, 1½ in. diam.
3 Porous earthen cups, 2 in. diam., 4 in. long.
2 Pipettes, bulb.
Pneumatic troughs (movable shelf for each basin).
1½ doz. Pinch-cocks, Mohr's.
12 Rubber corks, two preforations, for 12 oz. flasks.
40 ft. Rubber tubing, 20 ft. ¼ in.; 10 ft. ⅛ in; 10 ft. $\frac{3}{16}$ in.
3 Retorts, glass, 4 oz. Bohemian glass.
1 Retort, copper, 1 qt.
12 Supports, iron stands with two rings each.
12 Spirit lamps, glass globe shape; or 12 Bunsen burners if gas is used.
3 Sand baths, 4 in. diam.
1 Spatula, 5 in. blade.
1 set cork borers, 6 in a set.

EXPERIMENTAL CHEMISTRY

1 horn spoon.
10 doz. Test tubes; two doz. each of 4, 5, 6, 7 and 8 in.
2 Thermometers, 200 degrees Centigrade.
½ doz. Triangles, wire pipe stem covered.
1 doz. Test Tube racks, for 13 tubes, with drying pins.
½ doz. Test tube brushes, with sponge on end.
1 doz. Watch glasses, 2½ in diam.
1 doz. Wolff's bottles, two necks, 4 oz. each.
1 doz. Wire gauze 5 in. square.

INDIVIDUAL APPARATUS

Each pupil should be provided with the following apparatus selected from the preceding list:

1 Iron stand support with two rings and one clamp.
1 Test tube rack.
6 Test tubes.
1 Blowpipe.
1 Stirring rod.
1 piece asbestos
1 Piece wire gauze.
1 Watch crystal
1 ft. 6 in. Rubber tubing.
2 short pieces rubber tubing.
1 Florence flask with rubber cork.
1 Funnel tube.
1 Pinch-cock.
1 Pair forceps.
3 Glass plates.
4 Wide-mouthed bottles or cylinders (furnished by pupil).
1 Evaporating dish.
1 Beaker.
1 Glass plug.
  A few pieces of red and blue litmus paper.
1 Alcohol lamp or Bunsen burner.

PREPARATION OF SOLUTIONS.

(a) The common acids (sulphuric, nitric and hydrochloric), and ammonium hydrate purchased from dealers are concentrated. For ordinary use, unless otherwise indicated, they should be diluted by mixing with four times their volume of pure water. Small bottles (say, 4 oz.) of these reagents should be kept on the shelf over the student's table.

Great care should be taken in working with the concentrated liquids, as they attack the skin and often cause painful burns or ulcers. For this reason it is well for the teacher to prepare large bottles of the dilute solutions for the student to use in filling his reagent bottles. Small bottles of the concentrated acids should also be filled for the student's use.

(b) The following solutions are called for in the course. They should be prepared, filtered into bottles, and placed on the shelves for use when required. Use 30 to 50 grams in about 500^{cc} water:

Ammonium chloride, NH_4Cl.
Alum, potash, $KAl(SO_4)_2$.
Alum, ammonium, $(NH_4)Al(SO_4)_2$.
Alum, chrome, $KCr(SO_4)_2$.
Arsenic chloride, $AsCl_3$. (1).
Antimony chloride, $SbCl_3$. (2).
Barium nitrate, $Ba(No_3)_2$.
Barium chloride, $BaCl_2$.
Copper sulphate, $CuSo_4$.
Cobaltous chloride, $CoCl$.
Calcium chloride, $CaCl_2$.
Calcium hydrate, (lime-water) $Ca(OH)_2$.
Ferric chloride, $FeCl_3$.

Ferrous sulphate, $FeSO_4$. (3).
Lead nitrate, $Pb(NO_3)_2$.
Lead acetate, $Pb(C_2H_3O_2)_2$.
Mercuric chloride, $HgCl_2$.
Mercurous nitrate, $HgNO_3$. (4).
Magnesium sulphate, $MgSO_4$.
Potassium hydrate, KOH.
Potassium bichromate, $K_2Cr_2O_7$.
Potassium permanganate, $KMnO_4$.
Potassium Ferrocyanide, $K_4Fe(CN)_6$.
Potassium Cyanide, KCN.
Potassium chromate, K_2CrO_4.
Potassium bromide KBr.
Potassium iodide, KI.
Potassium nitrate, KNO_3.
Potassium chlorate, $KClO_3$.
Sodium chloride, NaCl.
Sodium nitrate, $NaNO_3$.
Sodium hydrate, NaOH.
Sodium carbonate. Na_2CO_3.
Sodium sulphide, Na_2S.
Strontium nitrate, $Sr(NO_3)_2$.
Stannous chloride, $SnCl_2$. (5).
Zinc sulphate, $ZnSO_4$.

(1) Treat the solid with a small amount of water; with much water it is changed into the oxide and hydrochloric acid.

(2) Called butter of antimony. Acidify the water with a considerable amount of hydrochloric acid. It may also be made by treating the metal antimony with hydrochloric acid containing a little nitric acid.

(3) Ferrous sulphate oxidizes when left in solution; it should be prepared as needed.

(4) Dissolve mercurous nitrate crystals in water acidified with nitric acid. It may be made by treating mercury with a small amount of dilute nitric acid.

(5) Acidify water with considerable hydrochloric acid. Pieces of metallic tin should be kept in the bottle to prevent oxidation to some extent. Fresh solutions should be prepared occasionally.

(c) *Ammonium sulphide*, $(NH_4)_2S$. See Experiment 39 (c) for method of preparation.

Hydrogen sulphide, H_2S. See method of preparation, Experiment 31.

Cochineal solution. Pulverize 4 or 5 grams of cochineal, add water, allow to stand for some time; then stir well and filter.

Iodine solution. Dissolve the solid in alcohol.

Indigo solution. Slowly add 2 or 3 grams of powdered indigo to about 10^{cc} concentrated sulphuric acid in an evaporating dish. Cover the dish and allow it to stand two or three days; and then add 500^{cc} water, stir well, and filter.

Litmus solution. Pulverize litmus cubes and add water; allow to stand for some time, stir well and filter.

ADDRESSES OF SUPPLY HOUSES.

Catalogues from the following houses have been received by the writer:—

JOHN TAYLOR & CO.,
    Corner First and Mission Sts.,
        San Francisco, Cal.

Also Agent for ZIEGLER ELECTRIC CO.,
    Boston, Mass.

ALFRED L. ROBBINS CO.,
    149 and 151 East Huron St.,
        Chicago, Ill.

BAUCH & LOMB OPTICAL CO.,
    515–543 North St. Paul St.,
        Rochester, N. Y.

THE CHICAGO LABORATORY SUPPLY & SCALE CO.,
    31–45 Randolph St.,
        Chicago, Ill.

HENRY HEIL CHEMICAL COMPANY,
    208–212 South Fourth St.,
        St. Louis, Mo.

F. A. BECKETT, Agent for HENRY HEIL CO.,
    220 Sutter St.,
        San Francisco, Cal.

Supplies may also be purchased of
SALE & SON'S,
    220 South Spring St.,
        Los Angeles, Cal

The author has had occasion to deal with John Taylor & Co., San Francisco; and with Alfred L. Robbins Co., Chicago. He has found both houses to be thoroughly reliable.

www.ingramcontent.com/pod-product-compliance
Lightning Source LLC
Chambersburg PA
CBHW020324090426
42735CB00009B/1394